*Conquer limiting beliefs and
pursue your purpose*

MASTER
YOUR
MINDSET

The Master's Way

Elizabeth Nader, Th.D.

Published by The Idea Woman, LLC
elizabethnader.com   coaching@elizabethnader.com

ISBN 978-0-578-48573-7

Library of Congress Control Number: 2019903617

About the Author

Elizabeth Nader is an author, entrepreneur, mindset coach, motivational speaker, and creator of the "Master Your Mindset" teaching series. In addition to a successful corporate career, Elizabeth cofounded several businesses, including two which have been ranked on the Inc 5,000 Fastest Growing Companies list.

She holds a Bachelor of Arts with a major in Business Management and a minor in Psychology, Master of Business Communication Certificate, and a Doctor of Theology. Elizabeth is a trained Elijah House Prayer Counselor and a Certified Life Coach.

Elizabeth has a passion for the intersection of her faith and biblical precepts with the principles of mindset, business, money, success, and destiny. She believes everyone is created intentionally with unique gifts, that, when discovered and put into practice, bring abundance to their life while transforming the world around them.

Her enthusiasm for overcoming obstacles and discovering purpose, love of entrepreneurism, energetic drive, and unwavering belief in people's potential propels her clients and students into new realms in both their personal and professional lives.

By far Elizabeth's most important role in life is that of dedicated mother to four precious children and partner to her husband in both marriage and business.

To my four wonderful children: Nicolas, Joseph, Noah, and Maia. Your childhood is too short to provide me with the time to tell you everything I yearn to, so I am grateful for the opportunity to capture some valuable advice in this book that I pray will be handed down to your children and beyond.

You are made of spirit, soul, and body. Don't just work on one area of your life. Aim to be strong spiritually, mentally, and physically.

I wrote this for you and your children. Remember that your first and most important source of advice, counsel, and wisdom should consistently be the Word of God and the voice of God. After that, I pray the guiding words of Mom and Dad always stay with you. I love you with all my heart and I can't wait to see God's purpose unfold in your life.

Be courageous and prosper!

To my mother, you have always been my angel on earth. We have been through many highs and lows together, but I would not be where I am today without your unwavering support. You never left my side no matter what happened, and I'll never be able to fully show you my appreciation for your undying love. You are one-of-a-kind and I adore you.

To my father, I pray the words on this page do your memory even the slightest bit of justice. My passion for this subject comes from you and the way you looked at life. The day I lost you I lost a profound influence and guiding light. You are, however, forever in my spirit and the spirit of my children. Your legacy is not lost but is growing in influence as a result of the Godly life you led in your short time on earth and the spiritual impact you will have on many generations. Thank you is not enough. I miss you.

To my husband, there would be no book if you didn't encourage me to step out and operate in my gifts. You've always been able to see the real me, especially when others just didn't get it. I came into a fuller understanding of who I am in God as a result of our marriage. I pray I can do the same for you. I love you.

Lori, thank you for hearing my heartbeat, embracing my message, and standing alongside of me. So excited for what is to come!

Lisa, your sweet mom told me a long time ago that I would write this book. How fitting for you to play a role! I will always miss her.

Table of Contents

↻RT "Controlling your mind and directing it to what you desire is the absolute basis for mastering your mindset and healing toxic beliefs…and of course changing your life for the better." @enaderofficial #purpose #perspective #motivation #mindsetreset #humility #mindsetmaven #mymtmw

↻RT "It is your mindset that will dictate the life you experience." @enaderofficial #mindset #attitude #mindsetisachoice #mindsetmatters #spiritualheart #mindofman #spiritsoulbody #choices #darkroom #mindisadarkroom #mindsetmaven #mymtmw

↻RT "How you see yourself and the world is created by authority, impact, and repetition." @enaderofficial #livebeyondlimits #selftalk #findingyourself #youarenotlost #mindsetmaven #mymtmw

↻RT "You can literally rewire your brain with your thought life, for better or for worse." @enaderofficial #first30last30 #thoughtlife #intentional #provision #healing #toxic #resistance #mindsetmaven #mymtmw

t♺RT "If we can distill life's purpose down to one goal, I submit that goal is simply to change someone's life for the better." @enaderofficial #purpose #findyourgift #lifesmeaning #pursuepurpose #purposeisaprocess #noshortcuts #successtosignificance #livewell #mindsetmaven #mymtmw

t♺RT "Achievement and significance do not come by chance, they are birthed through vision and tenacity." @enaderofficial #mymtmw #metron #strengths #servewell #kintsugi #branding #enhancethebreaks #mindsetmaven

t♺RT "If we want to attract more money and actually have it change us for the better, we need to work on our mindset first." @enaderofficial #mymtmw #moneymindset #startinside #individualism #healthymoneymindset #worth #generous #contentment #vision #motives #mindsetmaven

t♺RT "My failure is part of the fabric of my success, and one needs the other." @enaderofficial #mymtmw #failure #grace #blessings #countitalljoy #fallout #overcomingadversity #riseabove #learntolosewell #overcomer #endwell #endwhatneedstoend #rocky #mindsetmaven

Preface

Over 2,000 years ago, Jesus Christ claimed to be the son of God, the Messiah, and that He was the embodiment of all truth.

As both Billy Graham and CS Lewis are famous for saying, either Jesus was telling the truth, or He was a raving lunatic. I believe He was telling the truth. That is my worldview, and that is the filter through which I pass everything in my life: The Word of God.

I believe it is through Jesus and The Word of God (He is the Word) that we can uncover the wisdom and knowledge about how our minds work, how we overcome toxic mindsets, and how we can realize our purpose and experience our destiny in this world as we push past that which has held us back. I believe the Word is our source of power for true, lasting change in our lives.

William James, the father of American psychology, wrote often about the power generated by faith interacting with our subconscious (our spirit, our heart). It is through this intersection which I believe we will experience victorious living; therefore, I cannot teach about only our physical and psychological experiences in life without bringing in the element of faith and the One who knows how we function in spirit, mind, and body.

Whether you agree with my worldview or not, I invite you to read this book with an open mind and understand that the Laws of God, or as some say the Laws of Nature, will work for you regardless of whether you believe in Him who created both them and you. It is through applying the principles in this book that I pray, no matter your current worldview, you will uncover revelation that changes you and pulls you closer to the Revelator Himself.

I hold the same goal for you as the Apostle Paul had for the Colossians:

"My goal is that they may be encouraged in heart and united in love, so that they may have the full riches of complete understanding, in order that they may know the mystery of God, namely, Christ, in whom are hidden all the treasures of wisdom and knowledge." Colossians 2:2-3 (NIV)

I recommend that you always make it a point to uncover the worldview of anyone you allow to speak into your life...now you know mine!

Introduction

A good man always has to know his limitations,

but a wise man never sets limits on himself.

– Larry A. Fischer, my father

(inspired by Clint Eastwood's Dirty Harry character)

I have many memories of my father, a Clint Eastwood fan as well as a true master of his mindset, saying this to me when I was a child. The first part comes from a Dirty Harry movie, and the second part makes it a powerful life statement.

It is important to simultaneously realize what we don't know, while never placing limits on ourselves. There is a difference between having a healthy, powerful mindset that inspires you to constantly reach for your dreams, and that toxic attitude that gives off the impression that you know everything and have nothing to learn.

So why write this book, and why should you read it? At this point in my life I have succeeded and failed enough to understand what I know and what I don't know. I always say that one should never take advice from someone who presents a perfect picture of their journey...I am inspired by those who have been in the battle, bloodied and beaten along the way, who can point humbly to their successes, learn from their failures and constantly strive to reach a higher level. Those are people I want to be around, talk to, learn from, share with, mentor, and be mentored by.

The closer you get to the truth,

the simpler and more powerful the lessons become.

– Jon Gordon, The Energy Bus

Perhaps some things you read here will seem obvious and basic, but I have found in my coaching practice and in watching people "do life" that many are missing an understanding of the small things we do every day that create our reality, whether positive or negative. Many people go through life on autopilot and are unaware of the power they have to change anything in their life, no matter where they started or where they find themselves today. It is always your choice.

My calling is to draw out of others their potential and inspire them to reach for their dreams so they can step into abundance and transform the world with their unique gifting and purpose. I know that I am walking in my purpose because I absolutely love talking about, writing, and teaching this material to anyone who will listen. I just can't read, write, or study enough about the subject and am inspired by the simple and profound revelations I receive along the way. I am simply a messenger, giving you the message God gave to me and believing in doing so it has the power to change your life.

What can you expect from this book? You will learn about the one thing and only thing you have control over: your mind. Through the powerful definition of mindset, I will reveal what really controls your thoughts and how to identify and heal your double-mindedness. Understanding mindset allows us to then identify toxic thoughts and begin to change them. Once you are set free from limiting beliefs, you can more easily understand and pursue your unique purpose and influence in this world. We also deal with money mindset issues, which is one of the most critical challenges in most people's lives. Finally, the blessing of failure is explored and how to manage its inevitability correctly.

All things be ready, if our minds be so.

− William Shakespeare, King Henry V

The journey of exploration and learning should never end. Arriving is not the goal; it is about the richness of the journey. Thank you for making the choice to master your mindset and open your heart to ideas that can truly be life changing. If just one person lives a better life as a result of my efforts, my mission is accomplished.

Remember, for everything under heaven there is a PURPOSE. That includes you.

Selah

The thief does not come except to steal, and to kill, and to destroy.

I have come that they may have life, and that they may have it more abundantly.

– John 10:10 (NKJV)

Beloved, I wish above all things that thou mayest prosper and be in health, even as thy soul prospereth.

– 3 John 1:2 (KJV)

For a free copy of this book in electronic form, visit:
elizabethnader.com/ebook

CHAPTER ONE
The One Thing

Before you die, live the life you were born to live.

- Erwin Raphael McManus, The Last Arrow

We demolish arguments and every pretension that sets itself up against the knowledge of God, and we take captive every thought to make it obedient to Christ.

- 2 Corinthians 10:5 (NIV)

The One Thing

t is said that more people die Monday at nine in the morning than any other time. Is that because the start of the work week represents hopelessness instead of opportunity? Did these people know their purpose? Did they have strong direction in their life? Did they feel fulfilled and important? Did they believe they had choices or any control over what they experienced?

This statistic bothers me, and it should bother you. I open this first chapter with the quote from Erwin Raphael McManus because too many people never live the life they were born to live. Why is that? I believe it has everything to do with our mindset.

There is nothing else we can control in life but our mindset. Why does one person experience success while another flounders? With all of the differences in life, backgrounds, circumstances, opportunities and more...the one thing, the only thing, we can truly control is our mindset.

What is mastering your mindset all about? It is the process of dealing correctly with the things that **HAVE HAPPENED** to you, and that which **WILL HAPPEN** to you, so what is **SUPPOSED TO HAPPEN** to you, **HAPPENS**! It's all about experiencing the fullness of your destiny.

Remember the biblical story of the Israelites wandering in the desert for 40 years after being released from slavery in Egypt? If you don't know the story, read about it in the Old Testament. They were miraculously released from over 400 years of bondage in Egypt, and then led out of that land of pain and torment towards Canaan, a land flowing with milk and honey that God promised to them.

Their release from slavery was miraculous, but then their toxic mindset got in the way when they faced their first challenge. In fact, with almost every challenge the Israelites encountered in their desert trek on the way to their breakthrough, they had a bad attitude. They were negative, whining, complaining, ungrateful, and idolatrous. The result? They wandered in the desert for 40 years, instead of just taking a walk for only eleven days, as most scholars say should have been the length of their journey from Egypt to Canaan.

Not only did they suffer much longer than necessary, but only two men from that generation made it into the "promised land." Talk about a cautionary tale! Be careful, don't allow a toxic mindset to delay, or even make you miss, your destiny.

Beware the level of your expectations.

You may just reach them.

Whenever I teach a series on mindset, I start by asking my students what they hope to get out of the class. There are always a variety of answers, but most have the same theme. What follows is a sampling of those anonymous, verbatim responses from a wide variety of age groups. Perhaps you will see yourself in a few of them.

"I hope to get a different perspective than what I've heard my whole life growing up. Because I've heard everything from a spiritual perspective which is awesome and just fabulous. But sometimes I'm definitely naïve to the way that the rest of the world operates so I need to know about that."

"What I hope to get out of it is I guess a new perspective, a new mindset towards things, a new way of looking at things that I didn't see quite before."

"I'm dealing with some recurring issues in my life and I can't seem to overcome them. I know I need to change the way I think and approach life, but I just don't know where to start."

"I thought it was like how to focus, align your thoughts with the truth and to see people in a truthful perspective and myself in a truthful perspective. In situations not just letting thoughts from the outside, from others, and from the enemy, dictate my actions. I was hoping to get out of it to be able to touch other people's lives through teaching them the truth and to be able to find my real purpose."

"I think what I guess I'm looking to get out of it is maybe a deeper sense of what direction I really want to head in. I feel like I'm still at that stage of I don't know what I want to be when I grow up."

"I think what you've been given, what you are going to be giving everyone is literally jet fuel, and I look forward to that."

"I struggle with thoughts that seem to hold me back. I really don't know where they come from or how to overcome them. I know if I don't start to deal with these issues effectively, I'll continue to be stuck."

"One thing I've noticed a lot lately is how important our brain is and just the things that we think. So, I guess I was thinking that this would be a way to focus on our thoughts that will dictate our future."

"I believe that the majority of what's being fed to the majority of the people in our age group since we've been born is utterly backwards and garbage from what the actual truth is."

Before you dive into this book, think about what you expect from it and from yourself. Make a commitment to read it within a certain amount of time, and to do all of the suggested exercises. Write in it, dog-ear it, highlight it, and re-visit it as much as you need to until it sinks deep within your heart.

Don't kid yourself. Be honest with yourself.

Take your own inventory.

— Jack Canfield

At this point, this book has at a minimum piqued your curiosity or, on the other end of the continuum, you may be desperate for a breakthrough in your circumstances. Either way, the starting point is to be honest with yourself about where you are TODAY. Not where you think you should be, not where you wish you were, not the image you create on social media, and not what others expect of you.

My first ground rule is honesty with yourself. Once you commit to that, then you have to be aware of the "I know that already" attitude that can easily crop up. I've noticed sometimes people can become indignant to certain subjects and nod their head as though nothing I'm saying is new. When you feel that way, I ask you "OK, where is the breakthrough in that area of your life? If you know this already, then why are you not walking in victory? Why do you keep coming up against the same mountains?"

It is one thing to "know" something and entirely another thing to actually put it to work in your life and experience lasting change. The saying that "knowledge is power" is quite misleading. The truth is that the only power that exists in knowledge is when you apply it to daily living. Just knowing the truth but not acting on it is empty and meaningless. Let's change the saying to "applied knowledge is power". Yes, this book may contain common knowledge, but is it common practice in your life?

Be aware of when you feel threatened or defensive about something you read. If that happens, it is usually a signal to stop and dig deeper. It is a sign that you have some work to do in that area. You probably need to challenge old, toxic mindsets and strongholds, and the enemy of your soul, the resistance, will fight that process. It can be uncomfortable to do this work, but truly "no pain, no gain."

I'm sure you've seen this diagram before, but it is worth revisiting. If you don't get out of your comfort zone, you cannot expect change in your life! As a coach, I am called to be "sandpaper" in people's lives, to identify what needs to be adjusted and try to smooth out the rough spots. This can certainly be a painful process, but so important for growth.

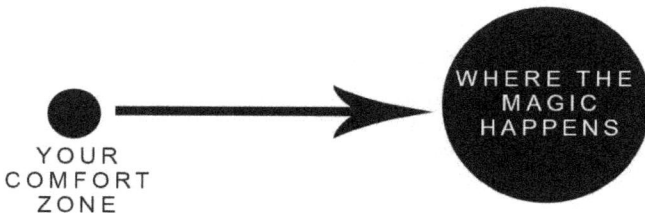

YOUR
COMFORT
ZONE

WHERE THE
MAGIC
HAPPENS

Are you aware of how a lobster changes its shell? It's a very relevant story for how we should handle stress and pain. The soft body under the lobster's shell grows to a point where the lobster becomes so uncomfortable that it must shed its old, smaller shell, so a new, larger one can replace it. As it goes through that process, it hides under rocks for protection while its new defense system is formed. This cycle repeats itself until the lobster is full grown.

Without that pain and discomfort, the lobster would never grow and never be forced to replace its shell. As Rabbi Dr. Abraham Twerski says, "If lobsters had doctors, they would never grow because as soon as the lobster feels uncomfortable, it goes to the doctor, gets a Valium, gets a Percocet, feels fine. Never casts off his shell."

Being uncomfortable usually precedes change, as long as you don't halt the process. Don't quit. Some of this information will be easy on you, some of it will be difficult. That's OK. Remember, you are not a victim of any situation in your life, you are actually a partner in the process. That means you have choices, but you also have to take responsibility.

Finally, forgiveness is an always present requirement in the process of healing your toxic mindset. It's not so much about who did what to you (although we will see that identifying the source of a self-sabotaging thought is often helpful), as it is about what your response was to the situation, with forgiveness being an important part of the equation.

Remember that having a healthy, winning mindset does not mean you will no longer have challenges or problems in your life. Those will always be with us, especially if we are reaching for our destiny - we will not live without resistance! But it does mean that you will have a powerful way to deal with the issues that arise in your life and experience victory in the midst of challenges. We are here to make each other's lives easier, so please share your breakthroughs and what you learn through this process to help someone else who is hurting.

There are two ways to be fooled.

One is to believe what is not true;

the other is to refuse to accept what is true.

– Soren Kierkegaard

In the study of mindset and the understanding of how it functions in our lives, it is necessary to examine the fact that we live in a world bound by God's Laws, or also called Natural Laws. Whether you believe in God or not, it is undeniable that our universe obeys certain laws that are immutable and unchangeable and don't depend upon your belief system in order to work.

By acknowledging that the world runs by these laws, we also acknowledge that our minds, our bodies, and our experiences are bound by natural laws as well. This knowledge allows us to leverage these immutable truths to our benefit as God intended and helps change our expectations about outcomes in our lives.

As a simple example, the law of gravity dictates that if I throw a ball into the air, it will naturally fall back to earth if it is within our atmosphere. I can vehemently deny this law and claim it to be untrue, but it won't make any difference or change the fulfillment of that law when I throw the ball into the air. My experience will be dictated by the law, not by my ignorance of it.

These natural laws are precise, many mathematical in nature, and most of them interdependent in some way. All of them must operate correctly in order for our universe to be possible. The following are some examples of these laws, which are referred to in the Bible as "ordinances of heaven and earth" in Jeremiah 33:25.

The Law of Life (Biogenesis) -Life always comes from life.

The Laws of Chemistry - Living things are powered by chemical reactions, elements and compounds have that logical properties.

The Laws of Planetary Motion -Kepler discovered that the planets in our solar system obey three laws of nature.

The Laws of Physics - Describes the behavior of the universe at its most fundamental level (like the law of gravity, mass, etc.).

The Laws of Mathematics - Physics only works because of the Laws of Mathematics, like the rules of addition, the transitive property, commutative, etc.

The Laws of Logic – One example is the Law of Non-contradiction: you cannot have both "a" and "not a" at the same time. According to the Bible, God is logical, He cannot lie or be tempted with evil since it contradicts His perfect nature.

The Uniformity of Nature - The Laws of Nature are uniform and do not arbitrarily change; they are the same in the past as in the future.

Where did these laws come from? I believe we have an intentional Creator and that natural laws are consistent with biblical creation. Astrophysicist Dr. Jason Lisle says, "Natural laws exist because the universe has a Creator God who is logical and has imposed order on His universe with laws that every living thing, every particle of matter or light wave, is bound by and has no choice but to obey."[1]

NATURAL LAW DEFINITION

(Webster's Dictionary)

NATURAL[2]

Inherent; having a basis in nature, reality and truth;

not made or caused by humankind.

LAW[3]

An existing condition which is binding and

immutable (cannot be changed).

This book is not about Creationism, so why is this important and what does it have to do with mindset? In order to better understand the forces that influence us, it is crucial to acknowledge that the world operates by all of God's laws whether the world believes in Him or not. For example, when we examine mindset, we understand that sowing and reaping, which is an immutable law of nature set forth by God, works in our lives whether we believe in the law or not. What we sow in our lives…what we focus on, what we meditate on, what we think about, what we talk about, what we give out to others…we will reap in our lives (the world also calls it karma).

There are laws that operate whether we recognize them or not, and then there are laws that exist for us to put in motion if we so desire. In fact, I believe that the world at large has "hijacked" God's laws and used them to prosper without even acknowledging Him as the source. Unfortunately, at the same time God's people have developed a fear of some of the language and secular ideas the world has wrapped around these laws. It seems it has even gotten to the point where we who were designed to prosper from God's laws don't even put them into motion in our lives. In some cases, we even allow them to work to our detriment!

As an example, let's look at the popular, secular Law of Attraction movement. If you believe that is New Age, don't get nervous, allow me to explain.

The Law of Attraction as the world sees it says that we have the ability to attract into our lives whatever we focus on, whatever we ask for. Many people have made millions of dollars by "selling" this law to the masses. If you analyze the concept, it is strongly biblical, and God told us about this Himself long before the world at large decided to embrace it as their own.

This is the 'you have not because you ask not' verse in the Bible…but notice it doesn't stop after the first sentence: "You do not have because you do not ask God. When you ask, you do not receive, because you ask with wrong motives, that you may spend what you get on your pleasures." James 4:2-3 (NIV)

Half a truth is often a great lie.

– Benjamin Franklin

The problem is the secular world takes the truth that God has spoken into existence and wraps it in a lie. So, while there is truth in secular philosophy, it ultimately has no redemptive power beyond the operation of the law itself. You may try to use the Law of Attraction to bring what you want into your life, but if your motives and desires behind your efforts are selfish and narcissistic, that eventually will bring pain and suffering to bear. This is not what God intended when He speaks of giving you the desires of your heart. In fact, the Bible says, "The blessing of the Lord makes one rich, and He adds no sorrow with it." Proverbs 10:22 (NKJV)

I recently watched a documentary on the Law of Attraction to gain a better understanding of how it is presented to the masses. While I don't remember one reference to God's Laws or Bible verses throughout the movie, God whispered a Bible verse to me for every concept presented. The longer I watched, the more excited I got that this Law was truly God's and should be embraced through the filter of His word in order to experience its life-changing power. In fact, understanding the Law of Attraction is a key understanding for mastering our mindsets.

When you hear the word "meditation," what comes to mind? This is another example of a concept that was meant to bless God's people and was taken by the world for their own purposes. It was

God's word first. There are more than 28 verses on meditation in the Bible, starting in the Old Testament. But when you say the word "meditate" outside of a church setting, some people misunderstand its purpose. Consistent faith-based meditation is one of the most powerful habits you can form. God revealed to Joshua the importance of meditation and how it would bless his life.

"Keep this Book of the Law always on your lips; meditate on it day and night, so that you may be careful to do everything written in it. Then you will be prosperous and successful." Joshua 1:8-9 (NIV)

Notice that God's way of meditating involves focusing on His Word (the Book of the Law). He does not instruct us to empty our minds as the world urges through various secular meditation practices. Worthwhile meditation does, however, require us to forgo our distracting thoughts and be intentional about on what or whom we will focus.

In fact, throughout the Bible you will find that an empty mind is a dangerous place that can be an invitation to be inhabited by our enemy or by toxic thoughts of our own creation. In scripture, we are given promptings on what to think upon, never to empty our minds or be devoid of thought. Yes, at times we need to be still so God can speak, but this is different than trying to achieve a state of no thought.

I believe that the application of Joshua 1:8-9 in our daily lives is not so much that we always quote scripture word-for-word, although that is powerful in itself, but that we live a life of constant meditation whereby God's thoughts, His words, and His promises as they apply to our life are consistently on our lips. We can choose to live a life where our response to every situation, every emotion, every blessing and challenge is to speak and respond from God's attitude and viewpoint. How do we know what that is? By reading His Word.

Everything you do, everything you say,

every choice you make,

sooner or later comes back around.

- Anonymous

As I mentioned before, sowing and reaping (or also known as The Law of Harvest) is another of God's laws that anyone can benefit from as it operates continuously in the physical and spiritual realm. When we think, speak, or act in a certain way, that has a direct correlation to what we experience in life through the Law of Sowing and Reaping. In fact, our speaking and acting flow from our thoughts, so that is why we focus on thoughts primarily in mindset mastering.

In the physical world, if I sow bean seeds into the ground, I will reap beans, not tomatoes. This is an understood Law of Nature, but it also operates the same way in our lives spiritually. If I sow godly, positive thoughts, I will reap godly, positive outcomes. If I sow negative, toxic thoughts, I will reap negative, toxic outcomes. You can ignore this law, but it will continue to operate whether you believe in it or not, so why not embrace it for your benefit?

Understanding the operation of this law also helps illuminate why we repeatedly face certain challenges in our lives. We must change what we sow in order to change what we reap. The main vehicle through which we do this is our mind and our thought life.

Those who cannot change their minds cannot change anything.

— George Bernard Shaw

I was blessed to be raised by a father who was continuously renewing his mind, focusing his thoughts, and sowing powerful things into his life, along with my dear mother. They certainly reaped a bountiful harvest as a result. My father was an entrepreneur, a salesman, a gifted orator, and deeply spiritual. I watched him build his business and his reputation by hard work, investing in those around him, giving generously, and having his priorities in order. But with all of this, I also witnessed him constantly reaching for new levels of self-improvement. My father started with nothing, and when his life ended suddenly at the age of 51, he was at the top of his career.

There was always studying happening in his den early Saturday mornings, for some new degree or licensing in his field. He didn't have the internet back then, so he had to proactively find things that would motivate and teach him to be more skilled at his craft and a better man as a whole. I can remember him listening to positive-thinking tapes (yes, cassette tapes), which could be found at all times in his office or in his car.

My father clearly believed in the godly power of positive thinking, and, besides studying the Bible daily, was an avid student of Napoleon Hill, Zig Ziglar, Dale Carnegie, Norman Vincent Peale, and others of his time. What I learned by watching his life had a profound effect on me, and in fact I believe my calling in life is in large part due to the investment he and my mother made in this area.

You either control your mind or it controls you.

– Napoleon Hill

The name of this chapter is "The One Thing." What is that? It is what forms the foundation for this entire book, the approach to mastering your mindset, and the basis from which I live my daily life and encourage those around me to do as well.

What is the one thing that God gave us absolute, total control over? There is only one thing. We do not have total control over circumstances, weather, economy, other people, the family in which we were born, our physical attributes, and on and on. We try to assert control in many of these areas, but the truth is we were not given, nor do we have absolute control over, anything except for this one thing: OUR MIND.

What does it mean to control your mind? You must understand how critical it is to assume this control, for you to control what happens in your mind as though it is the storefront of your entire being, which it is. It is the gateway to everything in your life, especially your spirit. Think of it as border security - what you allow in is what you become.

Why is "brainwashing" such a powerful, scary word? Because any time we give someone or something control of our thoughts, it results in control of our words, and therefore our actions. Guard your minds! Exert the control God gave you - don't just allow any thought to run around in there; it may just stay and set up shop. Controlling your mind and directing it to what you desire is the absolute basis for mastering your mindset and healing toxic beliefs…and of course changing your life for the better.

As this is the most fundamental concept for you to understand, I'd like you to watch an old video from Napoleon Hill on this subject. Who is Napoleon Hill? If you just asked yourself that question, I'm guessing you were born in the 1980s or beyond (or didn't grow up with my father). As my friend Lori says, Napoleon Hill is the "original Coke." He is the father of the 21st-century self-improvement movement and a man who has been imitated and quoted probably more than any of his peers.

Think about the well-known motivational speakers and writers you follow today. Without exception, and whether they realize it or not, I guarantee you their work is inspired by Napoleon Hill. This book itself and my worldview are greatly impacted by his insights. He is foundational to the idea of the power of mindset, and is well known for his book, *Think and Grow Rich*. All who have followed him have had their own unique take on the subject, but each is truly a "reboot" of the amazing intuition and inspiration of Napoleon Hill.

The video I'm recommending is old, but worthwhile wisdom never ages. In the video Napoleon Hill talks about an experience with his friend Dale Carnegie (another father of self-improvement) through which he was given the idea of the two envelopes. These two envelopes are the basis from which we operate in life. Envelope #1 is positive, envelope #2 is negative. Please pause reading now and watch the video on YouTube at this link:

https://www.youtube.com/watch?v=nBBZNE44Zow

If it is not found there, do a web search on "The two envelopes Napoleon Hill" to watch the video. The following is the transcript of the video if you are unable to find it:

> And it was in this field that I came upon a clue which has enabled me to help millions of people and their destinies. I want to describe my discovery in the simplest terms possible because it will reveal to you why it is true whatever the mind can conceive and believe the mind can achieve regardless of how many times you may have failed in the past or how lofty your aims and hopes may be. I caught my first fleeting glimpse of the profound law which provides the means by which we may choose our own purpose in life and attain it while I was being coached by Andrew Carnegie, during the organization of the signs of success philosophy.
>
> I just finished telling Mr. Carnegie that I feared he had chosen the wrong person to give the world the first practical philosophy of personal success because of my youth, my lack of education and my lack of finances. Well, at this point Mr. Carnegie delivered a lecture

that I shall never forget because it changed my entire life and paved the way for my helping to change the lives of millions of people, some of them not yet born. "Let me call your attention to a great power which is under your control" said Mr. Carnegie, a power which is greater than poverty, greater than the lack of education, greater than all of your fears and superstitions combined. It is the power to take the station of your own mind and direct it to whatever ends you may desire. This profound power," Mr. Carnegie continued, "is the gift of the Creator and it must have been considered the greatest of all of his gifts to men because it is the only thing over which man has the complete and unchallengeable right of control and direction. When you speak of your poverty and lack of education," Mr. Carnegie explained, "you are simply directing your mind power to attract these undesirable circumstances because it is true that whatever your mind feeds upon your mind attracts to you. Now you see why it is important that you recognize that all success begins with definiteness of purpose, with a clear picture in your mind precisely what you want from life."

Then Mr. Carnegie continued his speech with a description of a great universal truth which made such an impact upon my mind that I began then and there to give myself a new outlook on life and set up for myself a goal so far above my previous achievements that it shocked my friends and relatives when they heard about it.

"Everyone" said Mr. Carnegie, "comes to the earth plane blessed with the privilege of controlling his mind power and directing it to whatever ends he may choose." He continued, "Everyone brings over with him at birth the equivalent of two sealed envelopes one of which is clearly labeled: the riches you may enjoy if you take possession of

your own mind and direct it to ends of your own choice, and the other is labeled: the penalties you must pay if you would neglect to take possession of your mind and direct it. And now let me reveal to you" said Mr. Carnegie, "the contents of those two sealed envelopes. In the one labeled riches is this list of blessings: one, sound health, two, peace of mind, three, a labor of love of your own choice, four, freedom from fear and worry, five, a positive mental attitude, six, material riches of your own choice and quantity. In the sealed envelope labeled penalties," Mr. Carnegie continued, "is this list of the prices one must pay for neglecting to take possession of his own mind: one, ill-health, two, fear and worry, three, indecision and doubt, four, frustration and discouragement throughout life, five, poverty and want, and six, a whole flock of evils consisting of envy, greed, jealousy, anger, hatred and superstition.

Now my mission in life is to help you and everyone who needs my help to open up and use the contents of the sealed envelope labeled "Riches" and the starting point from which you must take off if you wish to write your own ticket from here on out for the remainder of your life. I will describe for you these simple instructions.

One, procure a neat pocket sized notebook or something on the order of this one here, loose leaf affair, and on page one write down a clear description of your major desire in life, the one circumstance or position or thing which you will be willing to accept as your idea of success and remember before you begin writing that your only limitations are those which you set up in your own mind or permit others to set up for you. And two, on page two of your notebook write down a clear statement of precisely what you intend to give in return for that which you desire from life and then start in right where you stand now to begin giving. And three, memorize both of your statements what you desire and what you intend to give in return for it, and repeat them at least a dozen times daily and always end your statements will this expression of gratitude for the blessings with which you were gifted at birth: I ask not for divine providence for more riches but more wisdom with which to accept and use wisely the riches I received at birth in the form of the power to control and direct my mind to whatever ends I desire.

If you are not too successful or self-satisfied to accept and express this profound prayer, if you accept it and express it in the same spirit of humble sincerity in which I pass it on to you and the better world will reveal itself to you. A world in which you will see reflected the circumstances and the things which you yourself have created. And now let me close this our first visit with my favorite expression of gratitude: Oh divine providence, I ask not for more riches but more wisdom with which to make wiser use of the riches you gave me at birth, consisting in the power to control and direct my own mind to whatever it is I desire.

- Napoleon Hill[4]

The envelope illustration is powerful if you meditate on it and put it into action in your life. At its basic level, all experiences in your life can be traced back to the direction of your mind to either positive ends or negative ends. It's not the circumstances you are changing at first, it is how you choose to experience them. Eventually, though, you will attract more positive circumstances in your life as a result of this mindset.

You will find in the "Mindset Shifts" section at the end of this chapter, an exercise in which you write out two envelopes as Napoleon Hill describes, along with an index card for each of the "penalties" or "riches" as detailed in the video. Keep these envelopes in eyesight until they become part of the way you grade your own thoughts and reactions. Ask yourself at the end of each day: was I mostly in envelope #1 or envelope #2? How could I have changed my reactions and thoughts to be primarily in envelope #1?

Parents, this is a great exercise to do with your children. Get them familiar with the concept and actually have the envelopes lying around where they can see them and interact with them. My children have been challenged by me many times, "Are you behaving out of envelope #1 or envelope #2 right now?". They have learned that their reactions, their thoughts, and their behaviors result in either blessing or cursing, all of which is under their control.

One of the tenets moving forward in this book is that you try to operate out of envelope #1 as much as possible. This will create an atmosphere where you are aware of your thoughts, what you are focusing your mind on, and how much control you are taking in directing the noise in your head. It is impossible to move from a toxic mindset to a powerful mindset if you live primarily out of envelope #2.

We've replaced attitude with entitlement.

– Lori Sica

The envelope exercise speaks to our attitude in life. At the end of this chapter I have included a famous quote from Charles Swindoll about attitude. My mother gave this to me at a young age and I have always tried to embody it. We are only in control of our attitudes, which is the same as our mind. It is our choice how we react to life's events, but of course it is not always our decision what happens to us. Our response of attitude is a choice.

Unfortunately, I believe we are seeing less and less focus in our culture on controlling our attitudes and directing our minds. Instead, there is a growing sense of entitlement in many of our youth which is borne out of a generation of parents who sought to give their children better lives and easier paths than they had, without realizing the downside and eventual harm it causes. We must learn that insulating children from failure or pain ironically sets them up for greater failure and pain in adulthood.

This entitlement environment removes the responsibility off of the individual for what they experience in life and places it in the hands of greater society. In other words, people with entitlement don't want to assume charge of their attitudes; rather, they want all good things handed to them without effort and without struggle. What is the ultimate result of this worldview? Disillusionment, pain, stymied purpose, and general malaise toward life. The responsibility for our attitude is ours and ours alone; no one owes us an easy path.

Continue to learn with humility not hubris.

Hubris is boring.

— Jimmy Iovine

As you learn more about fixing your toxic mindset, I challenge you to check yourself every now and then and ensure you are approaching this work from a spirit of humility and not hubris. Why? Humility is what allows us to be honest with ourselves and therefore we have a better chance at uncovering the true issues behind our thinking. Hubris, however, can cause us to believe falsely that our toxic mindset does not originate from our own choices and attitudes, but rather outside factors bear sole responsibility. There is no chance for healing if we hold an attitude of hubris.

Looking more closely at the definition of these words helps us see why choosing humility as we work on our mindset is so important. According to Webster's dictionary:

> **Humility**[5] = *freedom from pride or arrogance: the quality or state of being humble*
>
> **Hubris**[6] = *exaggerated pride or self confidence*

Hubris comes from the Greek language and is a prevailing theme in much of ancient Greek literature where we see characters experiencing tragic downfalls as a result of their hubris. The Bible even talks about it in Proverbs 16:18 (NKJV), "Pride goes before destruction, and a haughty spirit before a fall."

A good example in modern storytelling is the movie *Jurassic Park*, in which scientists decide to play God by using DNA to re-create long-extinct creatures. If you've seen the first movie or subsequent ones, you know the outcome was disastrous. A line that struck me from the first movie was what Jeff Goldblum's character said to the mastermind behind Jurassic Park regarding the re-creation of these dinosaurs, "Your scientists were so preoccupied with whether or not they could, that they didn't stop to think if they should."

Humility, on the other hand, represents a sober and accurate self-assessment. It takes a tremendous amount of courage to walk in humility, especially when we examine our mindset. Self-reflection and taking stock of where you really are can be terrifying. Humility isn't just about being willing to admit what is wrong, but also identifying what is right without pride.

True humility should allow you to admit your weaknesses without shrinking from them, while acknowledging your strengths without becoming puffed up. Humility is accepting what God's word says about you, but false humility, whereby you operate as though you are not worthy, is actually rooted in a reverse pride. I know that seems counter-intuitive but consider when we pull way back from what God intended for us, when we behave as though we are not worthy of the blessings and healings He wants us to have, we are actually feeling sorry for ourselves. We are stubbornly and pridefully choosing self-pity, self-indulgence, and all that comes with that, demanding negative attention from others. There is not much room for gratitude to God or acknowledgement of His power and love with an attitude of false humility.

As you work on mastering your mindset, remember that hubris means living by a falsehood. Humility means living by a truth. Choose truth.

When we come to the end of ourselves, we come to the beginning of God.

– Billy Graham

As you already know, I've based my mindset research on my worldview that God created us and therefore what He says about us as His creation should be our first guide to how to operate successfully in this life. What does God say about mindset? Plenty!

On the following pages I've included several verses for you that talk about mindset in one way or another. There are many more, and I challenge you to find them in scripture. There is such revelation and truth in these words that are life-changing if you apply the knowledge they offer.

I believe God never intended for us to figure out this life all on our own. He has given us such rich insight into how our minds work and how to lead a successful existence while we are on earth. He wants us to be prosperous, be in good health, walk in our purpose, and experience our destiny. To do so, we must master the one thing He gave us control over: our minds.

✛

MINDSET BIBLE VERSES
(NIV, unless indicated otherwise)

James 1:5-8 If any of you lacks wisdom, you should ask God, who gives generously to all without finding fault, and it will be given to you. But when you ask, you must believe and not doubt, because the one who doubts is like a wave of the sea, blown and tossed by the wind. That person should not expect to receive anything from the lord. Such a person is double-minded and unstable in all they do.

Romans 8:5-8 Those who live according to the flesh have their minds set on what the flesh desires; but those who live in accordance with the Spirit have their minds set on what the Spirit desires. The mind governed by the flesh is death, but the mind governed by the Spirit is life and peace. The mind governed by the flesh is hostile to God; it does not submit to God's law, nor can it do so. Those who are in the realm of the flesh cannot please God.

Isaiah 26:3 You will keep in perfect peace those whose minds are steadfast, because they trust in you.

2 Timothy 1:7 For the Spirit God gave us does not make us timid, but gives us power, love, and self-discipline. **NKJV** For God has not given us a spirit of fear, but of power and of love and of a sound mind.

Philippians 2:5 In your relationships with one another, have the same mindset as Christ Jesus ... (KJV: Let this mind be in you, which was also in Christ Jesus...)

Matthew 21:21-22 Jesus replied, 'Truly I tell you, if you have faith and do not doubt, not only can you do what was done to the fig tree, but also you can say to this mountain, Go, throw yourself into the sea, and it will be done. If you believe, you will receive whatever you ask for in prayer.

Mark 7:20-23 He went on: What comes out of a person is what defiles them. For it is from within, out of a person's heart, that evil thoughts come – sexual immorality, theft, murder, adultery, greed, malice, deceit, lewdness, envy, slander, arrogance and folly. All these evils come from inside and defile a person.

John 10:10 The thief comes only to steal and kill and destroy; I have come that they may have life and have it to the full.

Philippians 4:6-8 Do not be anxious about anything, but in every situation, by prayer and petition, with thanksgiving, present your requests to God. And the peace of God, which transcends all understanding, will guard your hearts and your minds in Christ Jesus. Finally, brothers and sisters, whatever is true, whatever is noble, whatever is right, whatever is pure, whatever is lovely, whatever is admirable – if anything is excellent or praiseworthy – think about such things.

Romans 12:2 Do not conform to the pattern of this world but be transformed by the renewing of your mind. Then you will be able to test and approve what God's will is – his good, pleasing and perfect will.

Colossians 3:2 Set your mind on things above, not on earthly things.

Proverbs 4:23-25 Above all else, guard your heart, for everything you do flows from it. Keep your mouth free of perversity; keep corrupt talk far from your lips. Let your eyes look straight ahead; fix your gaze directly before you.

Luke 6:45 A good man brings good things out of the good stored up in his heart, and an evil man brings evil things out of the evil stored up in his heart. For the mouth speaks what the heart is full of.

2 Corinthians 10:3-5 For though we live in the world, we do not wage war as the world does. The weapons we fight with are not the weapons of the world. On the contrary, they have divine power to demolish strongholds. We demolish arguments and every pretension (high thing) that sets itself up against the knowledge of God, and we take captive every thought to make it obedient to Christ.

1 Peter 1:13 Therefore, with minds that are alert and fully sober, set your hope on the grace to be brought to you when Jesus Christ is revealed at his coming.

Matthew 15:10,11 Jesus called the crowd to him and said, 'Listen and understand. What goes into someone's mouth does not defile them, but what comes out of their mouth, that is what defiles them.

Deuteronomy 30: 15-16 See, I set before you today life and prosperity, death and destruction. For I command you today to love the Lord your God, to walk in obedience to him, and to keep his commands, decrees and laws; then you will live and increase, and the Lord your God will bless you in the land you are entering to possess.

James 3:9-12 With the tongue we praise our Lord and Father, and with it we curse human beings, who have been made in God's likeness. Out of the same mouth come praise and cursing. My brothers and sisters, this should not be. Can both fresh water and salt water flow from the same spring? My brothers and sisters, can a fig tree bear olives, or a grapevine bear figs? Neither can a salt spring produce fresh water.

Mark 11:24 Therefore I tell you, whatever you ask for in prayer, believe that you have received it, and it will be yours.

Romans 7:22-23 For in my inner being I delight in God's law; but I see another law at work in me, waging war against the law of my mind and making me a prisoner of the law of sin at work within me.

James 4:2-3 You desire but do not have, so you kill. You covet but you cannot get what you want, so you quarrel and fight. You do not have because you do not ask God. When you ask, you do not receive, because you ask with wrong motives, that you may spend what you get on your pleasures.

1 Corinthians 2:16 (KJV) For who hath known the mind of the Lord, that he may instruct him? But we have the mind of Christ.

MINDSET SHIFTS

1. Meditate on the mindset Bible Scriptures.
   - What do they mean to you?
   - How can you apply them to your life now?
   - Can you find more?
   - Write a few on cards and put them where you see them every day.

2. Start collecting mindset quotes and meditate on them daily.

3. Create your own set of envelopes as illustrated in the Napoleon Hill video:

   Label Envelope #1

   The riches you may enjoy if you take possession of your own mind and direct it to ends of your own choice

   Envelope contents (one line on each of six notecards):
   1. Sound health
   2. Peace of mind
   3. A labor of love of your own choosing
   4. Freedom from fear and worry
   5. A positive mental attitude
   6. Material riches of your own choice and quantity

Label Envelope #2

The penalties you must pay if you neglect to take possession of your own mind and direct it to ends of your own choice

Envelope contents (one line on each of six notecards):

1. Ill-health
2. Fear and worry
3. Indecision and doubt
4. Frustration and discouragement throughout life
5. Poverty and want
6. Envy, greed, jealousy, anger, hatred and superstition

4. Put your envelopes in a visible place and be aware of your daily behavior

- At the start of your day, consider how you can choose to live as much as possible out of envelope #1.
- At the end of your day, ask yourself: How often were you in envelope #1 today?
- What could you have done differently to stay out of envelope #2?

5. Always strive to improve so you can claim the blessings in envelope #1.

6. Teach the envelope system to two other people.

ATTITUDE

"The longer I live, the more I realize the impact of attitude on life.
Attitude, to me, is more important than the past, than education,
than money, than circumstances, than failures, than successes,
than what other people think or say or do. It is more important than
appearance, giftedness, or skill. It will make or break a company
…a church…a school…a home. The remarkable thing is we have a
choice every day regarding the attitude we will embrace
for that day.

We cannot change our past…we cannot change the fact
that people will act in a certain way.
We cannot change the inevitable.

The only thing we can do is play on the one string we have,
and that is our attitude. I am convinced that life is 10% what
happens to me and 90% how I react to it.

And so it is with you…we are in charge of our ATTITUDES."

- Charles Swindoll

CHAPTER TWO
Exploring Mindset

You can't go back and change the beginning,

but you can start where you are and change the ending.

– C.S. Lewis

You will keep in perfect peace those whose minds are

steadfast, because they trust in you.

– Isaiah 26:3 (NIV)

Exploring Mindset

What is mindset? It is the filter through which we each see and encounter life. It is as unique to you as your fingerprint, and is a complex compilation of your predispositions, your personality, and your experiences. The interactions you have every day with those around you and the moments in your life, even those that are trivial, all impact the way you see your world.

It is your mindset that will dictate the life you experience. As children, our mindset develops mostly without our recognition or understanding. As adults, mindset is a series of choices you make every day, choices to interpret your world through the filter you maintain. You may not think of it as a choice, but it is.

As outlined in Chapter 1, the one thing you have control over is your mind and how you direct it. Therefore, it follows that you do have the ability to mold, adapt, and change your mindset as you see fit. You are not a victim of your mindset; rather, you are a partner in the process of how it develops.

In order to assume this control, it is helpful to have a strong grasp on the way mindset functions, its components, and how they operate in your life. Once you have that understanding, you can begin to make the changes that will allow you to master your mindset.

Your mindset matters.

*It affects everything – from the business and
investment decisions you make,*

to the way you raise your children,

to your stress levels and overall well-being.

– Peter Diamandis

The definition of mindset for the purposes of this book is:

> *A set of **BELIEFS** and*
> *a way of **THINKING***
> *that determine one's **ACTIONS***

At first glance this is a simple equation that reflects the source of our outward behaviors and actions. As we expand on it throughout this chapter, however, you will begin to see how significant and revelatory this definition of mindset actually is.

Our deeply held beliefs exist in our subconscious and create our reality. They make up our belief system that largely controls our life. Deeply held beliefs stream into our consciousness and create the majority of our thoughts, along with ideas that enter our mind from external influences. As a result of our thoughts, we act, we speak, we behave, we make decisions, we experience outcomes. It is all interconnected.

Beliefs plus thinking equal actions. To ensure you can visualize this connection, let's use two examples, one negative, one positive.

Example #1

Matt is a 45-year old professional who has a deeply held belief that money is evil, chasing it is greedy and inauthentic, and he deserves to lose anything he makes. That deeply held belief ends up in his conscious thoughts often and has become debilitating at his job and at home.

As a result, Matt makes choices in his life with the sense that "why bother, I'm going to lose it all anyway." He doesn't manage money well, is in debt, and he doesn't plan for the future. He has turned into a negative person, and his family finds it hard to be around him. Matt is cynical about anyone who has wealth and makes judgmental comments constantly. His finances are suffering, and he hates his job.

Example #2

Susie is a young actor just starting out, hoping to get a big break in Hollywood. All her life, her father has told her that she was something special, born to make a difference in this world and that she was immensely gifted. Objectively, her talents in performing are not overly unique, nor does she stand out as someone to remember. But Susie has a deeply held belief that she is meant to succeed and that her breakthrough is always around the corner.

She is positive, filled with hope, and takes every failure in stride. Her deeply held beliefs fill her mind daily with images of success and fame, and those thoughts guide her decisions and reactions to life. She begins to get small jobs and she senses a leading role is coming soon. Her tenacious spirit is starting to get her noticed in her industry.

In both instances, there is a deeply held belief that is at the core of the behaviors, actions, and experiences for both Susie and Matt. They may or may not be aware of the source of the belief, or even that it is in operation. But in both cases, that belief is in control, for better and for worse.

Thoughts are things,

and powerful things at that.

— Napoleon Hill

These two examples show a negative and a positive mindset, but both are mindsets of congruence, meaning the deeply held beliefs match the thoughts streaming in the consciousness of the mind, and therefore also the actions. What happens when there is incongruence, when the deeply held beliefs do not match the conscious thought life? That is when the challenge really begins.

Let's go back to Matt. Without focusing on where his deeply held limiting beliefs about money came from, let's just assume that the same ones are there. This time Matt has decided, however, that he wants to provide well for his family and makes every effort in his career to generate a comfortable income. His conscious thoughts are that he really wants to live a life with the safety net of money in the bank and save for his future. So why is he in constant lack, debt, and stymied at work?

Incongruence has become Matt's enemy. When your deeply held beliefs are at odds with your thought life, one has to win. You are sending out mixed signals - you say you want one thing, but you have a deeply held belief which is entirely opposite and is in control. No matter what you do, until you conquer that limiting belief, you are its slave.

The secular world says in this situation that you are sending out "chaotic vibrations" to the universe, and therefore the universe does not return to you what you say you want. I prefer to look at it through what our Creator says: you are double-minded and should expect to receive nothing. Yes, it's in the Bible.

James 1:5-8 (NIV) says, "If any of you lacks wisdom, you should ask God, who gives generously to all without finding fault, and it will be given to you. But when you ask, you must believe and not doubt, because the one who doubts is like a wave of the sea, blown and tossed by the wind. That person should not expect to receive anything from the Lord. Such a person is double-minded and unstable in all they do."

The Greek word for double-minded, diptychs, is the idea of a soul with conflicting information. That's exactly what is happening - your mind receives one set of information from your subconscious and deeply held beliefs, but your conscious thoughts are totally different. Conflicting information. Who wins? Your subconscious. More about that in a moment.

When you are double-minded, you have willed one goal in your conscious mind, but your subconscious mind has an opposite goal. The conscious mind may have the will, but the subconscious mind has the power. Power always trumps will. Thus, when you are in a state of incongruence and double-mindedness, you have no willpower, just a will with no power.

Double-mindedness:

the midway between dreams and realities.

— Ernest Agyemang Yeboah

Let's say you want to go on a diet. You've decided you are committed to losing weight and getting healthier, so you set out on this journey that millions have gone on before you. You are thinking positively, saying all the right things, buying the right foods, setting up your workouts, and just generally trying to create a structure for success.

The diet begins, and you start to see results. However, as soon as something stressful happens in your life, maybe with a relationship, or at your job or business, your will to stay on the diet starts to wane. You are up all night worrying, so you are too tired to workout. You start to fall away from your plans.

It happens to everyone at times, but for you it is a recurring cycle. You just can't stick with the regimen, and you begin to gain the weight back. What you are ignoring in all of this is your subconscious, your deeply held beliefs. You made a plan that included two of the three parts of your being, your conscious mind and your body, but you left out your spirit or subconscious.

If you spent the time to determine what limiting belief was keeping you from success in this area, you may discover that you were told your entire childhood that your family is all overweight and you will be as well.

Whenever you were sad, your mom gave you sweets and this started a connection for you of stress to poor eating. You were teased about your weight as a child, so you overate to insulate yourself from others.

Have you dealt with this pain and these limiting beliefs that are sewn into your subconscious? Probably not, and that is why you have no power behind your "will" to get healthy. As soon as an obstacle is encountered, you revert back to what is ruling in your life, your deeply held beliefs. You must do the work to heal those first (see Chapter 4).

Our aim is for our subconscious and conscious mind to be in concert with one another. What is the opposite of double-minded? Single-minded. This is what we must be. Have you heard the statement before, "He is very single-minded"? It is normally used as a compliment, to indicate someone who is focused and effective. We strive to be single-minded in all things.

If you want to succeed in anything you must change the goal in your subconscious mind to be in congruence with the desired one in your conscious mind. Then you have the willpower.

I realize that the following verse theologically is referring to the coming together with other believers in prayer, but I thought it interesting as it relates to double-mindedness. Matthew 18:19 (NIV) says, "If two of you agree on earth about any request you have to make, that request will be granted by my heavenly Father." Could the "two of you" be referring to our two minds? Our subconscious and conscious? Maybe a theological stretch, but interesting, nonetheless.

Don't believe everything you tell yourself.

God showed me something about the simple mindset definition of Beliefs + Thinking = Actions that took it to a much deeper level. We are created as triune beings...what that means is that we are comprised of spirit, soul, and body. We are a spirit; we possess a soul and we live in a body.

When you map this to the mindset definition, you start to see how everything is interconnected and why being in a state of congruence in your life is so important if you want to experience success, purpose, and destiny.

Your deeply held beliefs are in your subconscious, which is your spirit and also your heart (not the organ, but your spiritual heart. I will prove this to you with scripture). Your thinking is in your conscious mind, which is your soul and emotions. Your actions are exhibited in your body by your words and behaviors.

SPIRIT
Deeply Held Beliefs
Subconscious/Heart

SOUL
A Way of Thinking/Mind
Conscious Thoughts

BODY
Actions/Experience
Speaking and Behavior

Mindset and the Triune Being

When we see the interconnection between mindset and our triune being, we begin to really appreciate how important it is to take care of and nurture ourselves spirit, soul, and body. We must not be out of balance in any one area if we want to be healthy in all.

Let this always be a challenge to you: what are you doing daily in all three areas of your being to improve and grow? Are you feeding your spirit with prayer and meditation? Are you spending time to quietly connect with God and let Him speak to you?

How about your mind? Are you learning new things, stretching your abilities and challenging yourself mentally? Are you careful what you read and listen to? Are you managing your thought life?

Finally, are you taking care of your body? What are you doing daily to improve and maintain yourself physically? Are you eating well and drinking enough water to fuel your body and brain? Are you exercising and providing relaxation so your body can heal? Are you careful to get enough sleep?

There is so much we need to be doing to take care of our triune being. Make a commitment to yourself that you nurture each part of you in some way every day. If one area is out of balance or sick, it will affect the entire being.

As you consider the mindset definition and its relationship to our three part being, think about how each of the three aspects work and what they are responsible for in your life. Below is a chart to further define the differences:

BELIEFS +	THINKING =	ACTIONS
Spirit	Soul	Body
Heart	Mind	Speaking
Power	Will	Acting
Spiritual	Soulish	Carnal
Subconscious	Conscious	Outward
God-Consciousness	Self-Consciousness	Sense-Consciousness
God	Self	Senses
Relates to God	Relates to others	Relates to external
Revelation	Psychological	Physiological
Intuition	Reasoning	Effort

Body, soul, and spirit are interwoven with each other. Don't think of them as separate entities, but each one is part of the other. I have seen many graphics trying to depict this profound connection, but I offer you this simple image to help you understand how all three elements are interwoven.

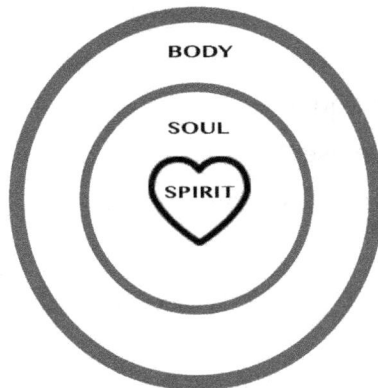

In His greatest commandment, Jesus teaches us to "Love the Lord your God with all your HEART and with all your SOUL and with all your MIND and with all your STRENGTH…and love your neighbor as yourself." Mark 12:30-31 (NIV)

This is a beautiful commandment which maps so amazingly to our triune being, and to the components of our mindset: Heart (Spirit), Soul (Mind), and Strength (Body). Jesus is telling us to use all three aspects of our being in our most important activity on earth: loving God, loving ourselves, and loving others.

The heart in the above graphic it is not meant to symbolize the organ of the heart, although that is certainly physically central to our being. This heart is the spiritual heart, or the hidden person of the heart as is mentioned in 1 Peter 3:4 (NKJV).

The mindset definition equates the subconscious to the spirit and to the heart of man. How do I know that connection is accurate? Only by looking at the owner's manual, the Word of God from the Creator of our being. He probably knows best how we function. Much of it is a mystery, but I can share the revelation through scripture and other sources that He has given me to support the notion of our heart equaling our spirit and subconscious.

As a culture, we use the word heart in our speaking in a way that reflects the attributes of our spiritual heart, as:

- The center of things (We need to find the heart of the matter)
- The place of deepest emotion (She felt the hurt deep in her heart)

- The center of hope and despair (We lost heart as the bad news came in)
- The center and source of worship (We sang to God from our heart)
- The source of pure and impure thoughts (He did the evil that was in his heart)
- The source of good and bad motives (In his heart he wanted to bless them)
- The location of the real you (At heart, he is a loving person)

In scripture, the word HEART is used at least 5,775 times. We see in the Bible that the heart yearns for God, it lusts and thinks evil thoughts, remembers and regrets, and feels hope, love, tenderness, woundedness, hopelessness, despair, fear, and pain.

Obviously, a muscle cannot have all of these attributes, but your subconscious/spirit can, and that is the seat of the heart of man. In fact, I will show you that your heart, and therefore your subconscious, actually has a mind of its own.

What is the subconscious? It is the seat of your automatic instincts that preserve you, those things that keep going and working even while you are asleep. The subconscious mind is comprised of thought patterns that run unconsciously due to your past experiences, successes, and failures. Every subconscious thought you have was once a "new thought" that you accepted and believed, which allowed it to be ingrained into your heart.

Most of us will spend more time thinking about our conscious mind, where we rationalize our experiences and make our choices. But our other mind, our subconscious mind, is actually the one which determines the decision for our choices, presents it to our conscious mind, and then the conscious mind forms the rationale for this decision. Therefore, the subconscious mind is actually in control the majority of the time, even though we may be unaware. The key is to bring the subconscious mind into harmony with the conscious mind.

The heart has its reasons of which reason knows nothing.

– Blaise Pascal

The idea that your spiritual heart has a mind may be a new one for you. But did you know that even the heart muscle, the actual organ itself, has its own "brain"? Scientists have proven that the more than 40,000 neurons in your heart can make their own decisions and decide how the heart responds to stimulation independent of your main nervous system.[1] Amazing how God imitates spiritual things in the natural.

As we look more closely at scripture, we can see where Heart and Subconscious can be interchangeable words, thus supporting the idea that the hidden heart of man is in the spirit, the subconscious. In the following you will find many scriptures with the word heart, where I have also included (subconscious mind) so you can read it either way.

These first three verses support the idea that who we are is based on our deeply held beliefs:

"For as he thinketh in his HEART (*subconscious mind*), so is he." Proverbs 23:7 (KJV)

"Above all else, guard your HEART (*subconscious mind*), for everything you do flows from it." Proverbs 4:23 (NIV)

"A good man brings good things out of the good stored up in his HEART (*subconscious mind*), and an evil man brings evil things out of the evil stored up in his HEART (*subconscious mind*). For the mouth speaks what the HEART (*subconscious mind*) is full of." Luke 6:45 (NIV)

"Rather let it be the hidden person of the HEART (*subconscious mind*), with the incorruptible beauty of a gentle and quiet spirit, which is very precious in the sight of God." 1 Peter 3:4 (NKJV)

"Trust in the Lord with all your HEART (*subconscious mind*) and lean not on your own understanding; in all your ways submit to Him, and He will make your paths straight." Proverbs 3:5-6 (NIV)

"Create in me a clean HEART (*subconscious mind*), O God, and renew a steadfast spirit within me." Psalm 51:10 (NKJV)

"And the peace of God, which transcends all understanding, will guard your HEARTS (*subconscious mind*) and your minds in Christ Jesus." Philippians 4:7 (NIV)

"...Do not let your HEARTS (*subconscious mind*) be troubled and do not be afraid." John 14:27 (NIV)

"Take delight in the Lord, and He will give you the desires of your HEART (*subconscious mind*)." Psalm 37:4 (NIV)

"Test me, Lord, and try me, examine my HEART (*subconscious mind*) and my mind." Psalm 26:2 (NIV)

"May these words of my mouth and this meditation of my HEART (*subconscious mind*) be pleasing in your sight, Lord, my Rock and my Redeemer." Psalm 19:14 (NIV)

I hope by now you are beginning to see how powerful your subconscious mind is and the critical role it plays in what you experience in life. In Mark 11:23-24 (NIV) Jesus says, "Truly I tell you, if anyone says to this mountain, 'Go, throw yourself into the sea,' and does not doubt in their HEART (*subconscious mind*) but believes that what they say will happen, it will be done for them. Therefore I tell you, whatever you ask for in prayer, believe that you have received it, and it will be yours."

Your subconscious works according to the Law of Belief. The Law of Belief states that it is not the thing that you believe in, but the belief itself that brings the results. In other words, if you believe something strongly in your subconscious (your inner game, your heart/spirit, your deeply held beliefs), you will eventually see that come true in your reality (your outer game). Beliefs are thoughts, and they are the power center, not the thing you are believing in.

Matthew 9:29 (NIV) says, "…According to your faith let it be done to you…". These were Jesus' words to the blind men whose sight he restored. He was speaking of their belief. When the Bible refers to belief, it is not talking about your belief in some ritual, ceremony, or institution. It is talking about the belief itself.

Your inner game dictates your outer game.

While you think, plan, and strategize in your conscious mind, what you believe on the inside, in your subconscious, is what dictates your reality. Deeply held beliefs dictate your thoughts, actions and habits, which of course result in your experiences.

Dr. Joseph Murphy, in his book *The Power of Your Subconscious Mind*,[2] says, "Your subconscious mind is a tape player that is not able to distinguish fact from fiction. If it is convinced that a false statement is true, it will act as if it were true. Your conscious mind, however, is your intellect, your thinking and your reasoning. It can accept or reject anything. So, if your subconscious is convinced you are a failure, it will make sure you fail. If it receives conflicting data, it will produce conflicting results. If it is convinced you are great and can achieve anything, you will achieve anything."

You will always act in ways that you feel or believe, not in ways you think. This is an example of how your subconscious has veto power over your conscious mind.

Once we understand this, the job of our conscious mind should be that of "watchman at the gate". You need to proactively engage in protecting your subconscious mind from limiting beliefs that can take up residence and control you. Sadly, most people are unaware of this and leave their gates wide open.

It's not just what we allow into our spirits and subconscious that becomes controlling in our lives, but it is also what we focus on with our conscious thoughts. I'm not sure who said it, but "that which you focus on expands" is eerily true. Try this fun example and see for yourself: start thinking about yellow Jeeps, or some other lesser seen color/car. Focus on them, think about them, imagine them. Guess what happens? You start seeing them everywhere! Be careful what you are focusing on.

I've always taken note of the scripture in Job 3:25 (NIV) that says, "What I feared has come upon me; what I dreaded has happened to me." In the context of our discussion of mindset, this is a cautionary statement to be careful what we fear, and what we allow to occupy our thoughts. Living in dread of a certain outcome means we focus on it, think about it, talk about it…and attract it to our lives!

Be wary what you feed your subconscious, what you willingly believe. As a child, we do not have the knowledge to be able to protect the things that drop into our spirits and take up residence. So, as adults, we are responsible for conquering those limiting beliefs and ensuring that we are not double-minded or allowing negative, deeply-seated patterns to control our lives.

The next two chapters will help you identify and heal the toxic thoughts that are holding you back. You must replace them with words and thoughts of life. What you focus on enlarges. Be inspired by Philippians 4:8 (NIV), "Finally, brothers and sisters, whatever is true, whatever is noble, whatever is right, whatever is pure, whatever is lovely, whatever is admirable - if anything is excellent or praiseworthy - think about such things."

Once your mindset changes,

everything on the outside will change with it.

— Steve Maraboli

By what process does a deeply held belief actually express itself in the outcomes of your life? There is a progression that begins in your subconscious, your heart/spirit, and ends up in the results of your life. I call that process The Mind of Man. This process also maps to our Triune Being: Spirit, Soul, and Body.

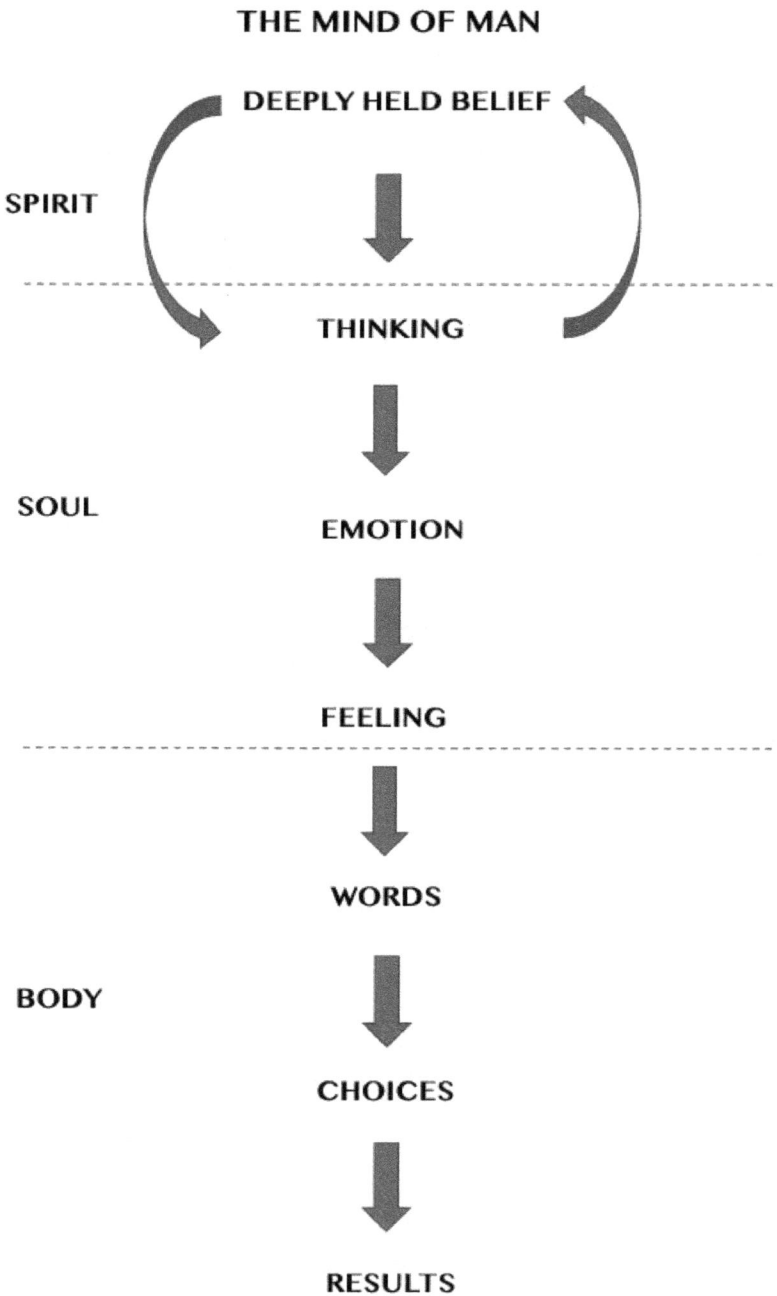

THE MIND OF MAN

DEEPLY HELD BELIEF

SPIRIT

THINKING

SOUL

EMOTION

FEELING

WORDS

BODY

CHOICES

RESULTS

The progression begins with the formation of a deeply held belief as a result of thoughts from experiences that you allow to drop into your subconscious. These may be positive or negative, but either way they make an impact in your heart that develops into a belief which will control how you see your world.

The thoughts can become deeply held beliefs, and the deeply held beliefs influence your thoughts. It is a cyclical process, and this is where you either create a limiting or affirming belief in your subconscious or challenge an existing one with new thoughts.

The thinking, emotion, and feeling stages represent your mind, your conscious, and your soul realm. This is where you do your reasoning and thinking and experience your emotions and feelings. You make choices in your will from your soul realm, and that is exhibited in your actions.

Your emotions are generated from your thought life. There are only two categories of emotions: faith or fear. All feelings emanate from either emotion; therefore, you are always operating in either a state of faith or a state of fear. The faith emotion is not necessarily rooted in spirituality for everyone; rather, it can be as simple as a positive belief or confidence in oneself. I have known people who have great "faith" but do not share my commitment to spirituality or God.

Additionally, do not assume that the emotion of fear will always appear as you expect; instead, know that fear can be a motivator behind feelings that mask as faith-based. Have you ever met someone with such confidence and swagger that you marvel at the faith they have in whatever it is they are doing? You would be shocked sometimes to learn that what you see is actually born out of a fear of failure or another fear, not blind faith in themselves.

Challenge yourself and look beyond what is seemingly obvious. Are your feelings (and therefore your words, actions, etc.) truly rooted in faith as you tend to assume? Or are they actually a product of masked fear? Finding this answer is often a breakthrough which helps people discover why their efforts to reach a particular goal in life are thwarted. We want to nurture true emotions of faith and act on them, not fear.

Emotions create changes in your body and feelings create changes in your mind. Feelings stem from assigning meaning to the emotion you are experiencing. I mention several times in this book how your feelings are a good sign of whether you are in fear or in faith, in envelope #1 or #2. Pay attention to your feelings because this is the point in the process where you can decide to go back to the emotion and then to the thought that created the feeling, or just go directly to the words and choices that affect your results.

When my children are exhibiting a negative feeling and don't seem to know why, I sit down with them to work backwards in this diagram. We examine which emotion is behind their feeling, either faith or fear, and then find the thought that created the emotion. It is here where we can challenge the thought, create a new deeply held belief or accept it all as is. This is where the work is done.

Feelings then impact your body, your words, your choices and ultimately your results. Your words are not random, they are rooted in feelings. Your choices are not independent, they are rooted in your words, which come from your feelings, emotions, thinking, and at the core, your deeply held beliefs.

You can see by this flow that your life experiences are a result of your deeply held beliefs and our deeply held beliefs are a result of our life experiences. The cycle is forever moving up and down the scale, and you can choose to interrupt the process and change it to your benefit at any time. You just need to understand how each affects the other so you can successfully conquer your limiting beliefs and begin to see positive changes.

This process should inspire you to control your thoughts, manage your emotions, understand your feelings, watch your words, and be wise about your choices.

Remember, the one thing we have control over is our mind and how we choose to direct it. That is why you do not see events or circumstances in The Mind of Man process; it is all about your reaction to what happens to you. All along, it is about choice. Choice is your greatest power to allow you to live a victorious life.

The mind is its own place.

It can make a heaven out of hell, or a hell out of heaven.

– John Milton

I am closing this chapter with a pointed passage from the book *The Power of Your Subconscious Mind*,[3] by Dr. Joseph Murphy. This book is full of such wisdom and encouragement and great insight into how our subconscious works with us or against us.

Your Subconscious Mind is a Darkroom

"Your subconscious is your great darkroom. It's the secret place where your outer life develops.

Therefore, it isn't your name, your manner of dress, your parents, your neighborhood, or the automobile you drive that makes you what and who you are. You are the beliefs taking shape, image by image, light and shadow, there in your subterranean darkroom. In a moral sense, your subconscious is totally neutral, willing to look on any habit as fitting, whether or not you or the world deems it good or bad. That is why when we blithely drop negative thoughts into our subconscious, into this darkroom of ours, time and time again, we are so surprised to see these dark thoughts finding expression in our day-to-day experiences and relationships…time and time again. As a matter of fact, it is rare to find something happening to us that we had no role in creating in this way.

In order for your world to change, you have to change your mind…from the inside out. But if you accept this darkroom concept you will find yourself happily free of emotion about the process. When you entertain this idea, you will find that changing your life won't be such a struggle. How much of an effort can it take to simply replace existing mental images with new ones? This understanding can mean the beginning of an easeful period of positive change for you.

It may surprise you to learn that all the beliefs and tendencies that were instilled in you from your earliest days are still with you, and they have power to manifest in and influence your life. All of us have many such beliefs and ideas that perhaps had their origins in childhood. These are hidden in the deeper recesses of this subconscious darkroom. Knowing this should make it clear why it's time to develop a healthy respect for your thoughts...If you fill your darkroom with great truths, your outer pictures will reflect them. Your subconscious mind will accept these truths...

Begin at once to think about whatever things are true, lovely, and noble, and you will see these qualities around you. Remember that God pronounced everything good and very good, and so should you. Thinking this way will give you a new, healthy reverence for your thoughts, and you will find that you will no longer be a victim of the pictures that you thought you had no part in developing."

✣

MINDSET SHIFTS

1. Think about areas of success as well as challenge in your life. Map specific experiences to the mindset definition to uncover the deeply held belief which is in control.

2. For the span of one week, write down the feelings you had during each particular day. Map each feeling to the emotion of fear or faith. Begin to see how much of our day is spent in which emotion.

3. With the knowledge, "that which you focus on expands," choose to focus on one positive aspect in your life day in and day out for a week. Reflect on how your experiences, feelings, and emotions changed during that week.

4. What is the most important thing you would like to see change in your life right now? Examine your words, feelings, emotions, and thoughts surrounding that situation. Create a plan to use The Mind of Man process to attract the results that you want.

Beliefs and The Law of Sowing and Reaping

If you accept a belief
You reap a thought
If you sow a thought
You reap an attitude
If you sow an attitude
You reap an action

If you sow an action
You reap a habit
If you sow a habit
You reap a character
If you sow a character
You reap a destiny

- Anonymous

Exploring Mindset

CHAPTER THREE
Identifying Limiting Beliefs

Beware of no man more than of yourself;

we carry our worst enemies within us.

— Charles Spurgeon

The heart is deceitful above all things, and desperately wicked; who can know it? I, the Lord search the heart, I test the mind, even to give every man according to his ways, according to the fruit of his doings.

— Jeremiah 17:9-10 (NKJV)

Identifying Limiting Beliefs

*O*nce you have a strong understanding of both the structure of mindset and how it operates in your life, the process of identifying limiting beliefs and toxic thoughts becomes a more significant and profound exercise. You now understand that thoughts are not just thoughts; rather, unchecked, they become deeply held beliefs that literally control your life experience.

Where do these thoughts, and subsequently deeply held beliefs, come from? Are we born with a pre-disposition to believe certain things? Do we have a genetic code that makes us more susceptible to fear or allows us to be greater risk takers?

How much of how we act and think is genetic or generational, and how much is learned behavior is mostly a mystery. General consensus is that both play a role in how we experience life. In some cases, we may be born with a genetic tendency that doesn't express itself until after a particularly traumatic or impressionable event occurs as a young child. In these cases, our experiences and our genes are truly interconnected. Without such an event, we may never "trigger" the expression of that genetic tendency in our life.

The focus in this book is on the one thing you can control, which is your mind and how you direct it. You cannot control the family into which you were born, or the genetic code that was handed down to you. Research does show us, however, that you may be able to alter that genetic code, or at least the expression of it, which we will discuss in the next chapter. First, though, you must identify the limiting beliefs operating in your life.

A lie repeated with authority, over time, is believed.

To identify the source of your deeply held beliefs, look to those in your life who have had the greatest authority or influence over you. Your beliefs come from parents, mentors, teachers, spiritual leaders, and other authority figures. Also, you can easily form a deeply held belief as a result of things you have witnessed and events that affected you strongly.

When you consider the "authority figures" in your life, remember that you can give authority to anyone and therefore allow them to impact your thinking. For example, if you desperately want to join a group of friends in middle school you tend to look up to them and give them a voice of authority in your life. Their acceptance or rejection of you therefore can have a major impact on how you see yourself.

The majority of your deeply held beliefs are formed in childhood due to the fact that you lack a functioning filter at that tender age telling you what to believe and what not to believe. Until the age of six or seven, children take in everything around them and are taught to accept ideas but not question them.

Not having the tools when you are young to protect your thought life leaves you susceptible to influences, voices, and experiences. In terms of your learned reactions, Sigmund Freud said, "We learn as children how to react emotionally and this is carried into adulthood. When we are children, we do not have the faculties that we do in adulthood. We do not know what we are going to need in adulthood to cope. Therefore, as adults we often react as children."

In other words, programs we learned as children were embedded in our subconscious mind and are still in control unless we willfully determine to change that programming. We don't realize as children that it is dangerous to our future to believe a particular thing or allow thoughts to go unchecked. We don't understand the price we will pay as adults, unless someone intervenes and teaches us to protect our thought life.

How you see yourself and the world is created by

authority, impact, and repetition.

As you identify limiting beliefs, you will find yourself focusing mostly on sources from your childhood but understand that this process can happen in adulthood as well, especially with traumatic experiences. For example, if someone goes through a difficult divorce, they may begin to believe they don't deserve love. You don't stop forming limiting beliefs until you decide to take control of your mind and your thought life.

Why is it so easy or natural for us to allow toxic thoughts to take hold? Why does everyone struggle with this on some level? Why do we have a tendency to hold onto limiting beliefs like a security blanket?

Ironically, I found the simple answer in a movie from the 1980's, *Pretty Woman*. Julia Robert's character is a prostitute, who is sharing with Richard Gere's character her life story and how she ended up in such a difficult place. She recounts how she trusted the wrong people who constantly put her down and eventually hit rock bottom. He tells her she could be so much more, that she is bright and special. Her response, "The bad stuff is easier to believe. You ever notice that?"

Wisdom from *Pretty Woman*, who would have guessed? But it's true! The bad stuff is easier to believe. Why is that? It is a simple case of your ego (the part of your personality that deals with reality), wanting to keep you safe. It is almost an automatic reaction that you must consciously override.

If you believe the "bad stuff," and it turns out to be true, you are safe, you don't look like a fool, and you don't have to feel like a failure. However, if you decide to counter the bad thoughts in your head and choose positive, affirming thoughts, you risk being wrong, you risk failure, and you risk looking ridiculous.

As an example, if you were told your entire life through voices and experiences that you will fail at everything you try, you have a choice to believe that thought or not. If you believe it, and you in fact fail at a new endeavor, you have not taken a great risk because you already knew that would be the outcome. But if you step out of your comfort zone, announce your plans to try something new, believe in your success, and still fail…well that is a disaster to your ego. So, your ego says, "stay safe, believe the bad stuff, don't risk being foolish and getting hurt."

Unfortunately, failure can happen anyway and is necessary as you will discover in the last chapter of this book. But how you see that failure is everything. In this case, if it further affirms your limiting beliefs, then you've stopped yourself once again. How will you ever know if your failure was a result of believing you would fail, or actually a necessary step towards your success?

A successful man is one who can lay a firm foundation

with the bricks others have thrown at him.

– David Brinkley

It is one thing to recognize a toxic thought as it travels through your mind, but how do you identify the deeply held beliefs in your subconscious that are incongruent with your thought life and your desired outcome? Look towards your feelings and the fruit, or results, in your life.

Remember from the last chapter that feelings are borne of one of two emotions: faith or fear. The feeling is the assigned meaning to the emotion, and feelings create changes in your mind.

When you are in congruence between your subconscious' deeply held beliefs and your conscious thought life, you will have feelings of joy, love, appreciation, gratitude, faith, trust, passion, enthusiasm, eagerness, happiness, positive expectation, optimism, hopefulness, contentment and more. These are your clues that you are in balance and congruence in that particular area of your life. Just like Envelope #1 living (see Chapter 1).

On the other hand, when your thought life is at odds with your deeply held beliefs and you are double-minded, you will be sabotaging your own efforts in that area and experience such feelings as boredom, pessimism, frustration, irritation, impatience, disappointment, doubt, worry, blame, discouragement, anger, resentment, revenge, hatred, rage, jealousy, insecurity, guilt, unworthiness, fear, grief, depression, despair, and powerlessness. Yikes. Not a great list. Sounds like living out of envelope #2, doesn't it?

You are what you do,

not what you say you'll do.

– Carl Jung

Not only do your feelings reveal double-mindedness issues in your life, but certainly looking at the results or "fruit" you are experiencing is a major sign as to whether or not limiting beliefs are sabotaging your efforts.

Why do we keep running into the same roadblocks? Why do we start, stop, and start again, only to continually fall short of our goals? When we don't see the results we want in our life, we need to look closely at what we truly believe, taking inventory of any deeply held belief that may be overriding all of our greatest intentions.

In Chapter 2 we discussed at length how the subconscious trumps the conscious realm anytime there is incongruence. Any attempt at starting something new in your life or changing old habits will be met with resistance, especially if you have limiting beliefs in control. Look at your life. Examine the results you are getting; are you seeing the kind of fruit you have hoped to see? Do the results reflect your mindset?

Being double-minded means we don't see the results we want or believe in our conscious mind we should have. There is nothing more telling than the measure of "fruit". We were made to be fruitful in our lives, we were made to achieve. If that's not happening, be willing to be honest with yourself so you can begin the work to identify the roots of the bad fruit.

Jesus said, "By their fruit you will recognize them. Do people pick grapes from thornbushes, or figs from thistles? Likewise, every good tree bears good fruit, but a bad tree bears bad fruit. A good tree cannot bear bad fruit, and a bad tree cannot bear good fruit.

Every tree that does not bear good fruit is cut down and thrown into the fire. Thus, by their fruit you will recognize them." Matthew 7:16-20 (NIV)

Words were first used for Creation,

not for Communication.

– Dr. Helen Trowbridge

Another very telling clue about whether or not a limiting belief is controlling an aspect of our lives are the words that we say. Words give us away and reveal not only what is in our minds, but more importantly what is held deep in our heart and subconscious. The Bible tells us, "A good man brings good things out of the good stored up in his heart, and an evil man brings evil things out of the evil stored up in his heart. **For the mouth speaks what the heart is full of.**" Luke 6:45 (NIV)

As a culture, we use words very loosely. We tend to say whatever comes to mind without a second thought or acknowledgement that words are powerful. Yes, they can hurt, inspire, encourage, diminish, rebuke, praise…the list goes on. But the most powerful aspect of words is their creative ability.

God first used words to create the world and mankind. We are made in His image, so it follows that our words would have similar creative force. In fact, He tells us, "The tongue has the power of life and death, and those who love it will eat its fruit." Proverbs 18:21 (NIV)

Can you create a star with your words? That seems silly, but consider that you can create your present, your future, and your every experience with the words that come out of your mouth. Remember the Law of Attraction? What if I told you that everything you have today, good and bad, is a result of words you spoke in days past? Would you be more careful about what you say?

Our words can keep us from the very things we want to achieve in life. As we will discuss more in Money Mindset in Chapter 7, I caution you to be careful how you judge other people's financial situations with your words. You will never have that which you criticize.

Your self-talk literally wires your brain to succeed or fail.

Go back to the progression chart in Chapter 2 which shows the flow from Beliefs to Results. Words are in that flow, after Feelings and before Choices and Results. And it's not just the words we say out-loud that have such power in our choices and the results we experience, but consider it is also very much the words we say to ourselves, in our head.

Your self-talk is the captain of your ship. It is the basis for your self-esteem and the director of the scenes of your life. Your self-talk has the power to create a foundation of success or failure for you. You must be careful of not only the words you say to others, but also the words you say to yourself.

When my second oldest son was seven years old, he had an

extremely strong sense of who he was. It was obvious to everyone and he seemed to be completely confident and in control of the impression he wanted to make on his world. When you spoke with him, he talked of big dreams and unlimited possibilities. It was fun to see him this way at such a young age.

About that same time, he had taken several "Hello" name tags from a party at our home and had written on each one a word or phrase about how he saw himself and his future. He did this on his own, and when I discovered them on the wall above his bed, I wasn't the least bit surprised. This was normal for him at that time to step out in such a bold way.

A few years later, things changed dramatically. Was it just in one day? Not likely, but something happened at school with someone in authority that made him start to question himself. Whatever that negative experience was, combined with the start of the tumultuous middle school years, changed my son. He no longer had the swagger of confidence but rather began to shrink from things at school and exhibit bouts of frustration never seen before. He even stopped wearing his signature bow ties and clearly wanted just to blend in and be left alone.

His dad and I were confused. What happened? It was gradual enough that we couldn't find a moment to hang our hat on, and to this day we can only guess as to the influences that made him question himself so strongly. I have several ideas, but I realize that it may not be just one thing, as it is usually a combination, a perfect storm.

During this time, we moved him and my oldest son into a

different bedroom in the house. While moving out their things, I found myself staring at that wall of tattered "Hello" stickers that had been there for four years. You could tell my son had unsuccessfully tried to remove them, but there they were reflecting another time when his self-image was clear, when he spoke into his future by positively declaring "Hello, my name is....".

I was so moved by looking at these stickers afresh now that my son was struggling to re-discover himself. It is precious to me, and I want to share it here with his permission. He has now come back to a stronger understanding of himself, but I will never forget how a young boy used statements of strength about his future to give him such confidence, until he began to believe lies from authority outside the home.

Take a look at the image and ask yourself what positive "Hello" statements you once had operating in your life that you have somehow lost track of. Do you need to get those back? Or perhaps you never had them and need to write them out as a guiding light to the future you want to live, to walk as the person God made you to be. It's time to write these statements.

Don't be falsely humble about this; rather, have the pure intentions of a child who knows he was created for something great. We all have been. Write those statements out on the blank name tags I've included at the end of the chapter. Look at them daily if you need to. Think of them as powerful "I am" statements.

 Don't let your negative words or the influence of negative authority steal your destiny.

My seven-year-old son wrote his nickname, and then:

> Hello, my name is: amazing person, profitable, successful, smart, cool, funny, meat lover, United States goal keeper with seven degrees

Your turn. What do you need to write?

We empower the lie we believe.

— Bill Johnson

What we say about ourselves and our circumstances is heavily influenced by the voices that we listen to. These voices can be external, coming from authority figures or others in our lives, or they can be internal and spiritual, originating in our own mind or from our enemy (resistance / Satan).

If we listen to a particular voice long enough without challenging it, we begin to internalize those points of view and lose perspective as to where the thoughts came from or why. We can even begin to protect the thoughts and refuse to challenge them, as we have become comfortable with what we tell ourselves, even if it is negative.

It makes sense that not only do we need to be careful about the words we say, but equally as concerned about the voices we listen to. Who do you want to be in agreement with? If you really understood the power of voices in your life that go unchecked, would you really listen to and agree with just any voice around you?

Our enemy is empowered by human agreement. Since his goal is to kill, steal, and destroy anything in our lives, we have to be wise to his tactics and understand that one of the most powerful tools he uses is to get us to agree with voices that are contrary to God's Word and what He says about our future.

Usually the most powerful voice is the one in our head. The one that runs 24/7 and simply won't shut up unless we take control over it and tell it what to think. Steven Furtick, in his book *Crash the Chatterbox*, calls this voice, the chatterbox,"…representing the lies we believe that keep us from accurately and actively hearing God's voice".

Yes, this voice may derive its content from the enemy of our souls or from others around us, but our biggest mistake is that we allow it to drown out the voice of God who is trying to speak truth to us. It is through our renewed spirit that we commune with and hear from God, but if our hearts and our minds are full of toxic thoughts and limiting mindsets, His voice simply won't make it through all of that clutter. Many of us don't even recognize or challenge the source of the voice we are listening to. We just allow the voices to drone on and on…

If you hear a voice within you say,

"You cannot paint", then by all means paint

and that voice will be silenced.

— Vincent Van Gogh

Research says we have more than 60,000 thoughts per day, and that the majority of those are negative…something around 80 percent.[1] That's a ton of limiting beliefs just running through our heads and impacting the life we experience. Think about what you could achieve in your life if you listened to or believed just ten percent less of the negative thoughts! How about 50 percent less?

Find those numbers hard to believe? Do your own research and pay attention to the thoughts you have in the span of just one hour. How many of them are negative? How many are self-affirming? You will be amazed at how many thoughts wander through your mind unchecked and unfiltered.

Your role in this never-ending battle with the voices in your head is to be the gatekeeper, to ensure that any negative, limiting thought that floats in be escorted out and replaced with a positive, life-affirming thought. This takes practice and intention for the rest of your life. As we established in Chapter 1, the one thing you have control over is your mind, and so it follows that it is solely your responsibility to keep your mind healthy and free of sabotaging voices.

Think of it this way - your mind is your storefront, your business, your enterprise. Would you allow just anything to go on in your store? Would you allow thugs to rifle through your merchandise, damage your property, or scream at your customers? Of course not. None of that negativity would be allowed in your store, yet you allow worse in your mind, unchecked, every day.

The voice you believe will determine

the future you experience.

− Steven Furtick

What's even more damaging than unfettered access to our minds is that we don't just allow the voices to have free rein, but we believe what they say! If the enemy can get us to believe the toxic, limiting thoughts, then he can keep us from our purpose and from our destiny, or from having victory in an area of our life. Every time we believe a voice contrary to truth, it makes it that much easier to believe the same lie next time it appears.

In fact, neuroscientist Dr. Caroline Leaf, in her book, *Who Switched Off My Brain?*,[2] explains the detailed chemical responses our body has to voices or thoughts that we believe. Our brain cannot distinguish between good and bad thoughts, so the same pathways are made as a result of the emotion that comes from a thought, and the memory of that allows the thought to be believed even more deeply the next time it enters our brain. In short, we create a home for that thought and make it increasingly easy for it to stay.

This is where the voices we listen to, the thoughts that we think, and the words that we say all tie together. As Dr. Leaf says, "The words you speak feed back into the magic trees of the mind, reinforcing the memory they came from. When you make negative statements, you release negative chemicals. These lead to negative memories that grow stronger and become negative strongholds that control your attitude and life."

We must make a conscious, concerted effort to be an effective gatekeeper of our mind and take charge of the voices that we listen to, the thoughts that we think, and words that we say if we hope to change the circumstances that we experience.

VOICES ──► THOUGHTS ──► WORDS

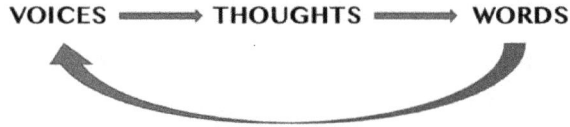

As we will discuss in the next chapter, you must consider your inputs in order to change your outputs. One aspect of this is the voices you listen to. Those voices, unfiltered and unmanaged, become your thoughts, and those thoughts, unfiltered and unmanaged, become your words. Your words create your reality and become one of the voices you listen to. The cycle is powerful in its ability to help you or hurt you.

On the following pages you will find many limiting belief statements that I have collected from people over the years. While it is a long list, it only scratches the surface of toxic things we tell ourselves. You may find yourself all over these pages, or you may find just a few, pointed statements which hit home.

Either way, as part of the exercise of answering "Where are you?" in step #1 of the next chapter, I ask you to go through the list at a measured pace, without distraction, and circle those that resonate with you. If you have others not listed, write them in at the end. You will then see exercises in the "Mindset Shifts" portion at the end of this chapter that will lead us into *Chapter 4: Changing Your Mindset*.

✝

LIMITING BELIEFS

I don't know enough
I don't have the time
I'm not enough
They'll think I'm greedy and inauthentic
They will find out I'm a fraud
I'm too weak
I don't have the right personality to succeed
I'll look ridiculous
I'm a failure
Women aren't supposed to be powerful
I lack focus
What if I fail?
I can't do this
I need to learn more
I'm not worth it
I never win - why even bother
I can't have it all
I can't handle it
My expertise is common sense
This is hard work
I don't have the skill I need
They will think I'm selfish and self-centered
Who would want what I offer
I can't afford to get help
I have nothing to offer
I'm not a morning person
I can't compete
They'll laugh at me
I have to be fake for them to like me
I'm already too scattered
I have to work too hard to succeed
I will spread myself too thin

I don't really need as much money as I think
Money makes people selfish
I'm not good at what I do
People won't like me if I'm successful
Now's not the time
Who do I think I am anyway
I don't have the money
I'll have to do a half-hearted job
My spouse will be envious if I'm successful
I tried before and failed
I don't have what it takes
It can't be easy - it must be hard
Who am I to do this
I'm not as good as she or he is
I'm too disorganized
My friends will judge me
I don't have all the answers
I won't have any fun
There is something wrong with me
I'm not understood
I'm not motivated enough
I won't be able to handle it
I won't be able to have a life
It will all be taken away when I get it
I don't want people to look at me
I just want to fit in
I'm not smart enough
I am not important
I don't deserve success
Why me
I'm afraid to fail
I'm not talented
Good things don't happen to me
I don't know what to do next
I could lose everything
I'm not good enough

I am invisible
I'm not interesting enough
I feel vulnerable
I can't stand up for myself
I finish last
I am a bad person
It's my fault
I'm ugly
I don't belong - I will always be on the outside
My feelings don't count - No one cares what I feel
I will always be lonely
The best way to avoid rejection is to isolate myself
I am the problem - it is my fault
I have messed up so badly I've missed God's best
If you knew the real me, you would reject me
I will never get credit for what I do
Men (women) have it better
Turmoil is normal for me
I will always have financial problems
I can't change
My value is in what I do
My best is not good enough
I have wasted my best years
I must be very guarded in what I say
I have to guard and hide my emotions
I hate being vulnerable
I just get used and abused
I have no will or choice of my own
I am out there all alone with no one to rescue me
I don't know what love is
God loves others more than me
God only values me for what I do
God is judging me when I relax
I have to stay busy
God has let me down - He may do it again
I can't trust God or feel secure with Him

When something is wrong, it is my fault
I can avoid conflict by being passive
I have to plan every day of my life
I can't relax
God shortchanged me
It is impossible to lose weight
I am stuck
I will always be fearful
I will always be angry
I will always be jealous
I will always be insecure
I will always be shy
The perfect life has no conflict
I can never meet the standard
I inherited these traits
My family has always been this way
I feel guilty when I spend money
I never have enough money
I will never be appreciated for my true self
I need to make other people feel comfortable
If you knew the real me, you would reject me
I am worthy only if I succeed
Money is only good if you give it away
I don't know what love is
I must do whatever is necessary to please others
I can't risk getting my heart broken
What if they don't like me
What if it doesn't work
I am completely under other people's authority
Authority figures will humiliate me and violate me
I can never meet the standard
When something is wrong, it is my fault
Too much time has passed
I'm too young or too old
I missed the boat
Something bad might happen

I've made too many mistakes
I don't deserve success
I can't save money
I need to be humble
Failure will be the end of me
I'll be embarrassed
I can't finish anything
My friends and family won't support me
I'm not special enough
Someone else already thought of it
It's OK to play small
People will think I'm arrogant

_____

_____

_____

_____

_____

_____

MINDSET SHIFTS

1. Without analysis, circle the limiting beliefs on the prior pages that you hold. Be honest with yourself and go with your first reflex.

2. Write down a RESULT that you'd like to accomplish in the next year or two.

RESULT:

_____

_____

_____

3. What is holding you back? Determine which self-sabotaging beliefs from the list you hold are keeping you from that achievement.

Write the top 3-5 below:

     1.

     2.

     3.

     4.

     5.

4. Who told you that?

Look at the top beliefs you wrote down in #2. Ask yourself:

- Who (or what) told you that?

- What situation reinforced it?

- If applicable, who or what situation continues to tell you this?

- What would happen if you chose not to believe it?

5. Write your powerful "I am" statements in the form of the "Hello, my name is" stickers included in this chapter.

Hello
my name is

Hello
my name is

Hello
my name is

Hello
my name is

Hello
my name is

Hello
my name is

Hello
my name is

Hello
my name is

FINDING YOURSELF

"Finding yourself" is not really how it works. You aren't a ten-dollar bill in last winter's coat pocket. You are also not lost. Your true self is right there, buried under cultural conditioning, other people's opinions, and inaccurate conclusions you drew as a kid that became your beliefs about who you are.

"Finding yourself" is actually returning to yourself. An unlearning, an excavation, a remembering who you were before the world got its hands on you.

- Emily McDowell

CHAPTER FOUR
Changing Your Mindset

Impossible is not a word.

It's just a reason for someone not to try.

— Kutless, What Faith Can Do

Let this mind be in you which was also in Christ Jesus,

who, being in the form of God, thought it not

robbery to be equal with God.

— Philippians 2:5-6 (KJV)

Changing Your Mindset

$\mathcal{T}$he process of discovering, identifying, and admitting to your limiting beliefs is often painful, but the exciting news is that you CAN change your mind! You have the power to choose to transform how you think, and therefore make a significant impact on your life experience. It is worthwhile work with tremendous potential.

Is change really possible? When young couples get married, often the advice given to them is "don't try to change the other person; don't expect them to change." Probably worthy advice that you marry someone who you actually love as they are, but at the same time, it's a bit depressing to accept that people will never change. Change is a choice, and it is not impossible! Make it your choice to change for the better daily.

Have you heard the term neuroplasticity? Webster[1] defines it as "the ability of the brain to form and reorganize synaptic connections, especially in response to learning or experience or following injury." Doctors who have observed this in action marvel at the power of the brain to change, to adapt, and to recover. We can harness this unique power of the brain to make changes in our mindset.

Limiting beliefs become emotional strongholds in your life and have a major impact on how your brain works. I recommend again that you read Dr. Caroline Leaf's work in this area to understand the powerful physical changes that happen in your body and your brain as a result of emotions, thoughts, and words.

Faith and fear are not just emotions, but spiritual forces with chemical and electrical representation in the body. Consequently, they directly impact bodily function.

– Dr. Caroline Leaf, Who Switched Off My Brain?

This proven connection between the chemical processes in your brain and the operation of your thought life will cause you to realize how critical it is to be cautious of what you think and what you allow into your subconscious. You can literally rewire your brain with your thought life, for better or for worse.

As discussed in Chapter 2, there are two groups of opposite emotions from which all feelings emanate: fear and faith. Every feeling you have is either based in an emotion of fear or an emotion of faith (or love). Everything you think and feel can be traced back to one of the two. Your brain reacts differently to each emotion.

When fear enters your mind, that thought causes psychological changes to your brain on a cellular level. The same is true for thoughts based in faith. Once a thought is received in your brain, it builds a memory around that thought that can either help or harm you. If you continue to entertain the thought, it will develop deeper patterns in your brain and become more easily accessed each time, and therefore harder to change.

Imagine what happens each time you experience a feeling or thought based in fear? Those pathways in your brain are created and unless you challenge and replace that limiting belief with a positive thought based in faith, it becomes a stronghold in your brain, both literally and spiritually.

Neuroplasticity says you can change how your brain is wired. Science supports the possibility that you do not have to be limited by your toxic thinking if you do the work necessary to replace those thoughts and emotions with ones based on faith.

Fundamentally, our life is determined not by genetics but by epigenetics. That is, the environment we live in and create for ourselves primarily determines the expression of our genes and our level of health.

– Dr. Louisa Williams

Besides neuroplasticity, you have the power of epigenetics to harness in changing your mindset. Epigenetics, defined by Webster's Dictionary,[2] is "the study of changes in organisms caused by modification of gene expression rather than alteration of the genetic code itself."

The leading-edge research in this growing scientific field shows us that how your mind perceives and interprets your environment does in fact control and manipulate your genes. It also acknowledges that mind and spirit, not just body, also play a role in who you are and how you experience life. Each has an impact on the other.

Epigenetics says that if we perceive events in a positive way, we can see positive results in our health and experiences, regardless of the genetic makeup we started with. The cells in our body can be reprogrammed by the chemical messages our attitude sends to them, thus changing the expression of our genetic code. This reprogramming can even turn diseased cells into healthy ones, or the opposite can be true, depending on the attitude.

It is interesting that people recognize patterns in their family in both behavior and health that tend to repeat generation after generation. We often don't challenge these patterns but imagine if one person decided to change their thinking, habits, health, or lifestyle in such a way that future generations of that family no longer repeat the patterns! Amazing to consider.

There is so much to learn and study in the area of neuroplasticity and epigenetics; I am simply opening the door for you to explore it further. Most importantly, understand that when you say it is impossible to change your thoughts, the direction your life is headed, the way things are "always done" in your family, your health, and your outlook on life....science says you are wrong! Science supports the idea that we can change, and that change can happen at the very cellular and genetic level. It really is a matter of choice.

The moment you change your perception,

is the moment you rewrite the chemistry of your body.

– Dr. Bruce Lipton

Now that you know you can make those powerful changes, you need to be aware of what tools, means, and methods will provide you the opportunity for lasting change, not simply a band-aid or a short-term reprieve. You know that science supports your efforts, but based on my worldview, I think it is critical to understand what God, the Creator of your brain, body, and spirit, says about it. What guidance does He give you?

Let's go back to the beginning, before everything on earth became so messed up, before man had to struggle with limiting beliefs. I personally believe in the literal story of creation from Genesis and that Adam and Eve were real, created in God's image. I realize some factions of my faith believe them to be an illustrative myth, but regardless, the story is very instructive to our exploration into God's method of healing our mindset.

As the story is told in Genesis, God formed a family for Himself through the creation of Adam and Eve. It says He created them in His image, which means that they were as perfect as He is, and everything around them in the garden was perfect...all things in harmony - no death, no sin, no destruction. No need for a book on conquering limiting beliefs and pursuing purpose.

Adam and Eve naturally had a healthy mindset, as does God. They did not have to guard their thought life as there was nothing around to impact them in any negative way. They communicated easily and fluidly with God through their spirits, so they understood who they were and didn't question their purpose or worth. There was no idea in them about shortcomings or fear of failure. They had it made.

HOLY

Enter resistance...the devil, the snake. The enemy of man was determined to break the connection between God and His creation by causing man to sin. He knew that God could not commune with sin, as God is a Holy being and cannot have relationship with that which is unholy.

What did the enemy do? Exactly what he does still today - he told a lie. Please read the story in Genesis if you are unfamiliar. Eve listened to the lie, literally swallowed the lie in the form of the forbidden fruit, and then convinced Adam to do the same. As a result of them going against God's word, sin entered the world, and broke their connection to a holy God; fear, shame and death were ushered into a previously perfect environment.

After they believed the lie, all Adam and Eve could see were their shortcomings. They hid from God because they suddenly saw their nakedness and felt the shame and guilt that sin brings. Everything around them became a world full of limitations and regret.

BROKEN

God must have seemed so far away. Can you imagine having such easy access to the heart and mind of God, to walk and talk with Him, and then to lose that completely? What a tragic loss, all because of a lie believed. Ever since that fateful moment, man through the centuries has sought ways to reach God, to understand Him, to define Him and to be like Him. It is a never-ending search to fill the God-sized hole in our hearts left by sin.

My theology tells me that God knew this would happen, and He had conceived a plan before the foundations of the world to restore His creation to Him. I'm going to make this theologically light, as this is not a book on theology, but let's just say that God had to make a way to put man's spirit back in communion with His spirit, and only Truth could do such a work of restoration.

As a result of the sacrifice of His Son, Jesus, the price was paid for our sin and the relationship was restored with God, through the cross. God sees us through the cross, which allows his holiness to commune with our sinful nature. We are restored through Christ.

RESTORED

The Bible states that the sacrifice Jesus made allows us to be the righteousness of Christ (we are seen by God as righteous) and to have the Mind of Christ. It is the Mind of Christ that shows us how we can restore our mindset and conquer our limiting beliefs, God's way.

I want to know God's thoughts.

The rest are details.

— Albert Einstein

Philippians 2:5 (NKJV) says, "Let this mind be in you which was also in Christ Jesus." The NIV of the same verse says, "In your relationships with one another, have the same mindset as Christ Jesus."

What is the Mind of Christ? Scripture makes it clear that there are seven aspects (see Isaiah 11:2 NIV):

Spirit of the Lord (the supernatural power source that creates God's thoughts in our hearts)

Spirit of Wisdom (all of God's supernatural thoughts themselves)

Spirit of Understanding (God's personal illumination of those thoughts)

Spirit of Counsel (God's personal instructions for godly choices)

Spirit of Might (God's supernatural ability to perform those thoughts in our lives)

Spirit of Knowledge (seeing God's thoughts manifested in our actions)

Fear of the Lord (walking in God's love and truth, fleeing anything that would quench His spirit in our life)

Compare this list of the seven attributes of the Mind of Christ to the Mind of Man as detailed in Chapter 2, and you will see the contrast of the nature of God to the nature of man after sin entered the world. We have the opportunity to layer the Mind of Christ on our natural ways of operating, which activates power and change in our lives.

Mind of Christ	Mind of Man
Spirit of the Lord	Deeply Held Beliefs
Spirit of Wisdom	Thinking
Spirit of Understanding	Emotion
Spirit of Counsel	Feeling
Spirit of Might	Words
Spirit of Knowledge	Choices
Fear of the Lord	Results

The seven aspects of the mind of Christ reflect God's divine nature (and by no coincidence, seven is the number of God and completion/perfection). When we grasp what we have available to us, it becomes clear we do not have to live under the curse of toxic mindsets and limiting beliefs; rather, we have the choice to participate in His divine nature, which makes a way when there is no way. We must understand, though, like everything else in our lives, it is a choice for us to "put on" the Mind of Christ. We must be intentional to do so.

2 Peter 1:3-11 (NLT) gives us specific instructions regarding

how to apply God's divine nature: "*By his divine power, God has given us everything we need for living a godly life. We have received all of this by coming to know him, the one who called us to himself by means of his marvelous glory and excellence. And because of his glory and excellence, he has given us great and precious promises. These are the promises that enable you to share his divine nature and escape the world's corruption caused by human desires.*

In view of all this, make every effort to respond to God's promises. Supplement your faith with a generous provision of moral excellence, and moral excellence with knowledge, and knowledge with self-control, and self-control with patient endurance, and patient endurance with godliness, and godliness with brotherly affection, and brotherly affection with love for everyone.

The more you grow like this, the more productive and useful you will be in your knowledge of our Lord Jesus Christ. But those who fail to develop in this way are shortsighted or blind, forgetting that they have been cleansed from their old sins.

So, dear brothers and sisters, work hard to prove that you really are among those God has called and chosen. Do these things, and you will never fall away. Then God will give you a grand entrance into the eternal Kingdom of our Lord and Savior Jesus Christ."

These verses encourages us to use everything God has given us to experience life the way He intended. Again, seven things are listed as additions to our lifestyles of faith (not fear): moral excellence, knowledge, self-control, patient endurance, godliness, brotherly affection, and love for everyone. I am so amazed and encouraged when I meditate on God's guidance and that He doesn't want mastering our mindset to be an unattainable mystery.

Your wound is probably not your fault but

your healing is your responsibility.

— Eric Thomas

Once a false or toxic thought takes hold in your mind and you continue to knowingly or unknowingly reinforce it, you must intentionally interrupt the chemical process in your brain that cements those thoughts, and replace them with positive, life-affirming mindsets which have the power to re-wire your mind and subconscious.

There are practical steps you can take to change your mindset and eliminate limiting beliefs from your life. Like anything with staying power, it is a discipline which you must approach with commitment and honesty. It is a method by which you can "clean-up" toxic thought patterns from your past, as well as a way to deal with potential mindset pitfalls happening now or in the future. As I said in Chapter 1, mastering your mindset is the process of dealing correctly with the things that **HAVE HAPPENED** to you, and that which **WILL HAPPEN** to you, so what is **SUPPOSED TO HAPPEN** to you, **HAPPENS!**

After much meditation and paying attention to what works in my life and others, I created fourteen steps in the process to conquer limiting beliefs. The fourteen steps put into action much of what we have discussed already. In the back of this chapter you will find all fourteen steps listed in brief order for your reference.

#1. Where are you? Weary, Wounded, or Wrecked?

The first question God asked Adam after he and Eve listened to the deceiver and went against God's commands was, "Where are you?" Do you really believe God didn't know where Adam was? Clearly an omniscient God does not need to ask us questions, but I believe He purposely asked this of Adam to force him to be honest with himself and identify where he was.

We need to ask ourselves the same question as we set out to conquer our limiting beliefs. Where are you? Locate yourself and your toxic thoughts. Be honest about the struggles in your life, be willing to tell yourself the truth about where you need help, and have an accountability partner. Find someone you are comfortable being open with. You don't need to air your dirty laundry with everyone, but don't do this alone.

Look at what's not working in your life, and admit to the limiting beliefs and negative emotions attached to each issue. This is the work you should have done in Chapter 3. You can't fix what you don't acknowledge, so you must answer the "Where are you?" question with as much transparent honesty as possible, understanding the pain that may accompany that confession.

When I first started teaching this material, I used to move on to step #2 after explaining how we need to be honest about our limiting beliefs. Soon, however, I realized that it wasn't as simple as just the identification of a lie we were believing. God showed me there was also a spectrum, a progressive scale on which we could each find ourselves in relation to a specific toxic thought. Depending on where we were on that gamut, it would require different levels of healing to set us free.

Before we move on to the rest of the thirteen steps, you need to find yourself on this spectrum:

Weary   -   *Wounded*   -   *Wrecked*

Other words for this continuum are: Bruised, Broken, and Burned Out. It is a progression that you move along when limiting beliefs and lies are not dealt with properly in your life.

We have all been weary. Times in our lives where we feel like we are faint of heart, that we just can't seem to make it through, when we are tired of dealing with the same issues, the same challenges. We appear to be OK to others, but we drag ourselves through our days.

Weary is the early stage; think of it as though you are dealing with a head cold or a virus that you caught. The next step, however, is more like a visit to the emergency room - you are wounded. You feel bruised, hurt, impaired, or injured and cannot function as you normally do. Perhaps what you were dealing with at the weary stage has now developed into a more serious problem because you ignored the symptoms.

Being wounded requires more intensive help. Without intervention and opportunities for healing, you then risk heading to the wrecked stage, where now you are in the ICU. Your spirit is crushed, and your heart is broken. You are in many ways on life support in your emotional and thought life.

Without realizing it at the time, I watched this progression take place in the life of a dear friend whom I loved very much and who ended up taking his own life. Many of us tried to help him with his struggles, but sadly the lies he was believing and the voices in his head convinced him of things that made it virtually impossible to reach him with the truth. I look back now at this tragedy and realize how critical it is for us to answer "Where are you" with not only admitting to the limiting belief that is holding us back but also recognizing how far we are in the progression of our response to the lie that has been controlling us.

There is hope for each stage: weary, wounded, and wrecked. But you need to recognize it in yourself and others in order to provide the appropriate care...much like they do in triage, where the patient is assessed and handled medically according to the seriousness of their wounds. When we see where we are, we can apply the necessary level of intervention, work, prayer, and commitment to keep us from traveling too far down the continuum.

WEARY

As discussed before, feelings give us a good sign of what is happening in our heart and subconscious. A weary person is tired, dragging, downcast, melancholy, sorrowful, troubled, unhappy, weakened, and just generally lacking spark for daily living. Everyone deals with this off and on in life.

Feeling weary? Begin to work on countering the lie you are believing that is trying to rob you of your joy. At this point doing the work in this book can prevent you from developing a wound.

This is the most common place we all find ourselves in; we must recognize it, address it, and do what is needed to stop its progression.

At the weary stage self-care is often the most helpful: getting more sleep, trying to remove unnecessary commitments, exercising, eating right, praying/meditating, spending time with friends, asking for and extending forgiveness, etc. This type of care, in addition to countering the limiting belief that brought us there, is often enough to keep us from being wounded.

"Do you not know? Have you not heard? The Lord is the everlasting God, the Creator of the ends of the earth. He will not grow tired or weary, and His understanding no one can fathom. He gives strength to the weary, and increases the power of the weak. Even youths grow tired and weary, and young men stumble and fall; but those who hope in the Lord will renew their strength. They will soar on wings like eagles; they will run and not grow weary, they will walk and not be faint." Isaiah 40:28-31 (NIV)

WOUNDED

A wounded person is often resentful, offended, agonizing, stymied, miserable, blaming, mournful, impaired, tormented, confused, sensitive, damaged, hurt, and powerless. A wounded person refuses to counter the lies they are believing or do the work to extend forgiveness to themselves and others. Consequently, they are at risk for developing a bitter root of judgment which then brings with it many of the feelings listed above (sounds like envelope #2 living, right?).

Wounds are harder to hide than weariness. In fact, wounds often need to be exposed in order to heal correctly. They must be cleaned out and not covered up too quickly to ensure no infection takes hold. Expose your wounds to people you trust as a way to start your healing process.

As you go through the steps in this chapter for conquering your limiting belief, recognize that you are actually in a wounded state regarding that lie and understand that the work to heal it may be more intensive and take more time. The steps are the same, but the commitment is greater.

If you are wounded in your spirit, seek to heal the wound by all means necessary and monitor it to make sure the healing progresses and it doesn't fester and turn into a bigger issue. Don't hide your scars, they are a healthy reminder that you survived a wounding and confirmation that you can heal again in the future.

"But I will restore you to health and heal your wounds, declares the Lord." Jeremiah 30:17 (NIV)

WRECKED

A wrecked individual can be seen as having a crushed or slumbering spirit. At this stage your deep emotions are not functional, and there is little communication between your spirit and your mind. Because of the direct relationship between our spiritual health and our physical health, our bodies become obviously affected and we have more difficulty overcoming illness or disease.

It may be at this stage where mental illness materializes in the form of depression, crippling anxiety, disassociation from our spirit, and feelings of being cut off from our true self. Things that are broken or crushed do not operate the way they were created to, and a wrecked spirit means our triune being (our spirit, soul and body) are not working together the way they were designed.

When you have a crushed spirit, everything you do comes from the soulish realm. All of your emotions are soulish, all decisions are carnal without the guidance of the spirit, your instincts are often wrong, your reactions to other people are off, and it seems as though you have lost your guiding light. Your creativity has disappeared, and you struggle with worship, meditation, or personal devotions.

You can operate in life with weariness and woundings, but you cannot operate a normal life with a crushed spirit. A wrecked, crushed, slumbering spirit struggles to commune with God. It is as though your spirit is asleep. This is the stage of a broken heart, where your heart is your spirit man, or your subconscious.

A wrecked spirit must re-awaken to God. More intensive care is needed to heal from this state and the limiting belief underlying it. Often your inner child needs to be ministered to, and forgiveness of yourself and others becomes even more crucial. There may be heavy spiritual forces at work that need to be addressed such as generational curses, demonic influences, or the operation of the occult. The damaging physical effects of this stage must also be addressed.

The steps in this book represent ongoing freedom from mindset issues, but a person at this critical stage must understand the depth of their wounding and those helping them must see it correctly and take the healing steps even more seriously.

"The Lord is close to the brokenhearted and saves those who are crushed in spirit." Psalm 34:18 (NIV)

#2. Who told you that?

The second question God asked Adam in the Genesis story after they ate of the forbidden fruit was, "Who told you that....?" in response to Adam saying he was naked and afraid. Nakedness was not something Adam had noticed about himself, not something he was ashamed of before sin entered the world. Suddenly now it formed the basis for a limiting belief, and God wanted Adam to recognize the source.

Discovering the source of a toxic mindset or limiting belief is not about blaming and pointing fingers. That would be counterproductive, as you will understand in the step about forgiveness. However, it does help to shed light on how a limiting belief took hold in your subconscious in the first place and continues to dominate. Jesus said when we have bad fruit, we need to identify and pull up the bad root.

The "who" or the source of the lie you have believed may be a person or an event. It may have happened in your childhood or more recently. It probably has been reinforced in different ways throughout experiences in your life. You may not remember the source or the situation, but I have found most people can point to something as the root.

Identifying the source may help you understand why you allowed the limiting belief to become truth in your life and should empower you to be able to challenge the lie and replace it with the right mindset. Often when we are able to see the event or the person from a place of maturity and with the distance of time, we can see how we reacted in a way that set us up for a negative stronghold in our mind.

Do not get stuck on this step or obsess over it. If you don't know the "who", perhaps you are not meant to at this time. Move on and do the other work; it may be revealed to you later when you are better able to manage the information. Do not use the excuse of discovering the source of a limiting belief to blame anyone; we alone are responsible for our choices and our reactions. That's hard to accept when we see our young selves, but taking responsibility is the primary way out of the toxic mindset.

Use this step to keep yourself from believing a lie in the first place. Our culture today has an ever-growing scourge of "fake news", way beyond just political topics. Social media has been the primary weapon of delivery, but the broader internet itself is full of lies and misinformation. "Who told you that?" is an even more urgent question to ask ourselves in this day of 24/7 information. We have to develop a habit of continually considering the source of anything we choose to believe. It is not so simple anymore just to read something, believe it, and "swipe" past it. Instead, you must be vigilant to find out who said it, why they said it, and ponder if you really should believe it. The truth is becoming harder to find, but more crucial than ever to keep us from developing limiting beliefs.

 # 3. What has it cost you? What will it cost you in the future?

We tend not to make changes in our life unless we understand that not doing so will continue to cost us something. Yes, we avoid working on our issues because we want to escape the associated pain underlying the problem, but most of us recognize there is an ongoing cost to our lives by not doing so.

At this step, it is helpful for you to consider and admit to the negative impact on your life of the limiting belief you are trying to change. Your past, your today, and your future have been or will be affected if you do not change. Take stock of that impact.

By believing the lie, what price did you pay in your past? What relationships were hurt, what good things went undone, what gifting of yours went unexplored? What is happening right now in your daily life as a result of this limiting belief? Do you have a lack of sense of purpose? Are you empty and unfulfilled? Have you abandoned dreams and relationships that mattered? Do things feel broken? Are your closest friends and family suffering because of this lie?

Think about your future. What will believing this toxic thought steal from your future? Will your dreams be possible? Do you see yourself walking fully in your gifting and purpose? Will what you do in your life make a difference for someone else? What price will others pay in the future if you continue to hold onto this limiting belief?

If you can be honest about the cost, you will be ready to make the changes. Steven Furtick said, "When lies are not confronted, callings are not fulfilled."

#4. Decide: enough is enough!

It may seem obvious, but don't assume that your resolve is strong enough until you have truly settled in your heart that you are done with the negative impact of a limiting belief in your life. Life is all about choices, and at this step, you literally must be in agreement with yourself that you are done believing the lie.

This is the step where many people get stuck, because they often skip it or assume it is obvious. Consider how many people in your life continue to deal with the same recurring issues, the same challenges, the same problems. Think about your life. We were given the gift of free will, but often we don't intentionally exercise it for our benefit. Many times, we just default to doing nothing.

This is where my patience runs out, and why God gifted me to be more of a coach, not a counselor. Coaches point out to you what you need to work on and expect you to commit to that work and begin to see change. Counselors may do the same, but those gifted with the counseling spirit are often willing to continue to hear about the same issues time after time. They are wonderful listeners, patient and empathetic supporters. God bless them...I'm not wired that way.

Make a decision. Are you done with it? You can't change someone else's behavior or how they treat you, but you can decide to change your reactions, your thought patterns, your mind. The one thing you have control over - exercise that control! If you don't draw the line in the sand at this stage, you risk being stuck at steps 1-3 forever on whatever limiting belief you are trying to eliminate.

You will face resistance throughout this process, and we will discuss that more in detail in step #13. This is why a resolve to change is necessary because once you determine you want to move forward, it will seem as though everything pops up to try to stop you. Your resolve and commitment to yourself will keep you going, with God's help. Enough is enough!

#5. Visualize how life will change if you overcome this toxic belief.

In step #3 you were honest with yourself about what this limiting belief has cost you in the past, in the present, and what it will cost you in the future. Now in this step it is important to clearly visualize what your life could look like without the limiting belief. Be detailed and specific; it may be helpful to even write a few paragraphs about the experiences you are having in your life once the toxic thoughts have been removed. What have you been able to accomplish? What do your relationships look like? How are your finances? How is your health? What dreams are coming true?

This is not time to be falsely humble. Be bold about the great possibilities that wait for you once you overcome the limiting belief. You must give your brain a word picture to reach for, one that will keep you motivated when the old habits and thought patterns want to return.

Writing down the vision for your life is a powerful exercise and one that I believe you should practice continuously. I love the following verse in Habakkuk, as it speaks to the importance of writing down your vision and holds the promise that while it is for the future, it will not tarry, but will come to pass. How exciting!

"Then the Lord answered me and said: Write the vision and make it plain on tablets, that he may run who reads it. For the vision is yet for an appointed time; but at the end it will speak, and it will not lie. Though it tarries, wait for it; because it will surely come, it will not tarry." Habakkuk 2:2-3 (NKJV)

#6. Ask for and extend forgiveness and open your spirit to God daily.

If I had to pick one step that, if skipped, will keep you from conquering your limiting belief more than any other, it would be forgiveness toward anyone in your life who helped plant a negative belief in your spirit. Unforgiveness is the prison we build for others that we end up living in ourselves.

Unlike trust, forgiveness does not need to be earned. We are commanded to extend it, and without doing so, we end up entrapping ourselves. The Bible says that we receive forgiveness according to the forgiveness we give. The irony of unforgiveness is that it defiles me and everyone under my influence, but it does nothing to the person against whom I hold a grudge.

From the world's point of view, we have every right to withhold forgiveness from those who have hurt us, especially those who have caused us to believe a lie that has held us back. But we cannot be controlled by the sins of others; we are only responsible for how we choose to react to what is done to us. It is OK to be angry, but we must not sin through unforgiveness.

Bitterness towards someone distorts our perspective, and a distorted perspective will keep us from understanding and seeing the truth. Does forgiveness require we restore all relationships? Not necessarily. We must release the people who have hurt us, but we do not have to pursue relationship with them if it is not safe for us. That decision is between you and God.

Don't forget to forgive yourself in this step. We are often our worst critics and are not quick to give ourselves a pass for our mistakes. Ask God to forgive you, forgive others, and forgive yourself!

Finally, in this step keep your spirit open to God daily. Allow Him to work in your heart and continue to show you what is true and what is a lie. Submission to God will keep our hearts protected and our feet on a straight path.

"Therefore submit to God. Resist the devil and he will flee from you. Draw near to God and He will draw near to you. Cleanse your hands, you sinners; and purify your hearts you double-minded." James 4:7-8 (NKJV)

#7. Consciously control your thoughts.

God gave you control over your mind and how you direct it. Use this control and take responsibility for what goes on in your thought life. Don't let thoughts just run loose in your mind, but learn to engage interactively with each one. Is this a thought you want to accept or reject?

Be proactive and understand that if you allow negative thoughts to wander unchecked through your mind, they can develop a stronghold and become the basis for a limiting belief. Without managing and consciously controlling your thoughts, the bad thoughts have just as much of a chance of hanging around in your mind as the good thoughts.

There is a price to pay for not actively controlling your thought life. You must analyze each thought and decide if it stays or if it goes. But if you delay and ponder the thought, it begins to develop roots and it sets up shop. It will be much harder to reject the next time it comes to mind.

Is it really possible to analyze every thought you have? The practicality of it is questionable, but not every thought we have needs to be analyzed. You know which ones require management as they are the ones that form the basis for your limiting beliefs. They are the thoughts that continue to trap you in bad habits and painful cycles in your life. Sometimes you need to say out loud, "I reject that thought" and visualize yourself removing it and banishing it from the spaces of your mind.

"Finally, brothers and sisters, whatever is true, whatever is noble, whatever is right, whatever is pure, whatever is lovely, whatever is admirable - if anything is excellent or praiseworthy - think about such things." Philippians 4:8 (NIV)

#8. Watch your input and output.

Your output (your words and actions) are a direct result of your input. The input-output connection is something that mothers understand instinctively. As an example, when a child is irritable, or has a rash, mothers immediately problem-solve by thinking through what "inputs" created the output of the bad mood or rash.

An irritable child may have had too much junk food with dyes or sugar in it, and therefore his behavior is affected. Perhaps he missed a nap or is hungry. A rash is the body's way of getting rid of a toxic input, a sign that the body is trying to rid itself of an invader or irritator. Mothers understand that input is directly related to output. If you want to understand the output, find the input.

The same is true for your life. If you are seeing a result that you do not like, check the input. You need to function as your own gatekeeper and understand that whatever you allow in, will come out in some fashion. Without standing guard over our inputs, we will have no way to improve our outputs.

Jesus says in Matthew 6:22-23 (NKJV), "The lamp of the body is the eye. If therefore your eye is good, your whole body will be full of light. But if your eye is bad, your whole body will be full of darkness. If therefore the light that is in you is darkness, how great *is* that darkness!"

This is one of many scriptures in the Bible that talks about our eye gate, and others mention our ear gate. What we look upon and what we listen to gets inside of us and changes our output: our attitudes, our thoughts, our words, our actions, our emotions, etc.

What books do you read? Who do you listen to for guidance? What are you watching on TV or in the movies? What kind of people do you surround yourself with? It isn't that we want to become legalistic or isolated, but we need to be wise enough to understand that whatever we expose ourselves to becomes part of us, and those influences which are more frequent will especially show up in the fruit of our lives.

As we work towards eliminating toxic thoughts and limiting beliefs, we cannot be successful if we continually surround ourselves with "inputs" which support the negative thinking. We must change what we allow past our gates. If the source of a toxic belief is someone you love or are in a committed relationship with, be careful here. You must figure out how to protect your heart while you do this work but also honor your commitments unless it becomes unsafe or unwise for you to do so.

#9. Replace your negative statements and thoughts.

Once you identify a limiting belief, you need to replace that lie with a statement of truth. Much like the HELLO stickers my son made, you need to write out "I am" statements that speak positively, countering the toxic mindset you are trying to change.

When you challenge a thought in your head as part of step #7, you need to have something to replace that negative thought. It's not enough simply to deny the thought, but it must be replaced with a statement of truth that you can meditate on. This is the process of rewiring your brain.

The first line of defense is to replace your negative thoughts with positive, affirming statements. Then comes the battle of our words. Our words shape our reality, so begin now to watch what comes out of your mouth and actively replace your negative talk with the truth and the results you want to see in your life.

So few people have a guard over their mouth, and many don't

understand that what they experience in life is often a result of what they say. I heard the term "spiritual cutter" once and it gave me a visual of how many people's own words continuously "cut" their spirit and wound them, some to the point of disabling growth.

I had a student in one of my classes tell me about a trick he uses to keep himself from saying negative things and helps others to do the same. Whenever a negative statement is said, you have to add "and that's the way I like it" to the end of the statement. Amazing how quickly that puts into perspective what we are doing to ourselves with our words. Example: "I fail at everything I try, and that's the way I like it"...oh no! This exercise will change your words very quickly.

Be intentional about replacing your toxic thoughts and negative words. If you don't feel that you have truth to counter them, find scriptures that affirm you and your future. There are plenty. Write out "I am" statements and meditate on them. Have a vision for the outcome you desire in your life...think about it and speak it out.

#10. Choose love, express emotions, and develop nurturing relationships.

Galatians 5:6 says that faith works through love. That means that without love, our faith will not be effective in our lives. As you work to conquer limiting beliefs, you must choose to walk in love in your daily life and relationships to ensure your faith is effectual.

We are often taught as children to repress our emotions. Especially after traumatic events, our nature is to try to bury the emotions so we don't have to deal with the pain behind them. All this does is further lock us into a cycle of limiting beliefs, as emotions are real and alive, and burying them does not eliminate them.

If this is your pattern, learn now how to get in touch with your emotions. Expressing emotions does not mean you have to wear your heart on your sleeve or let everything hang out for anyone to see. Rather, you need to express emotions appropriately in an environment that is safe, accepting, and non-judgmental. Do not deny your feelings, acknowledge them, face them and deal with them as soon as you can. If you bury emotions, they will come back.

I've heard some people say that God doesn't want us to be emotional. I think that is wrong. He doesn't want us to be led by our emotions, but as He made us with emotions, they are not inherently bad. God's not trying to get rid of your emotions; He wants you to control them so they don't control you. Repressing them does nothing but long-term damage.

Finally, as part of this step think about your relationships. No man (or woman) is an island, and true heart work cannot be done without the support and nurture of special people in our lives. We need to be held accountable, but we also need to be loved and love in return. Don't isolate yourself in your struggles. Find your tribe, no matter how small, and invest in those supportive relationships.

#11. Practice daily prayer and meditation (First/Last 30 rule)
Re-establishing or deepening your communication with your Creator is crucial. You cannot do this work in your own strength, without supernatural support. Tapping into the greatest love this

universe has ever seen will give you the power and the stamina to do the work you need to overcome your limiting beliefs.

Most people who practice consistent daily prayer and meditation on some level will tell you that it is life-changing and brings a level of peace to your day that you wouldn't normally have. I believe you should start all prayer and meditation with expressions of gratitude, as it is an attitude of gratitude that has a unique way of focusing our thoughts on things that are worthy and puts our issues into perspective. Practice daily gratitude.

Everyone is so busy that it can be challenging to find time to quiet yourself and engage in prayerful acts, but when you are trying to upgrade your mindset, it is especially necessary. We somehow find time for the things that are important to us, so make the decision to allocate even a small part of your day for yourself in this area.

Consider this: what you spend the first 30 minutes or the last 30 minutes of your day doing can have a major impact on how you sleep and how you experience your day. I call it the First 30/Last 30 rule. Make a commitment to yourself that you will either pray, meditate, or just think on things that are positive, life-affirming, full of gratitude, and encouraging in both the first 30 and last 30 minutes of your day and see how life changes for you. This is a great place to speak your affirming statements that you created in step #9 to counter your limiting beliefs.

#12. Maintain a daily positive expectation.
The First 30/Last 30 rule gives us a framework to start and

finish the day with positivity and truth. What we tell ourselves is the most important. Our words create our reality, as we already discussed at length in previous chapters. Watch your words and get yourself in the habit of speaking life into your day. Create and maintain a positive, hopeful expectation especially during challenging times.

It may be helpful to use a daily mantra similar to the one below, which you can post around your house, memorize and repeat in your head or out loud, or keep handy on your phone for when you need to reset your expectations.

I am positively expecting great things in my life every day, no matter what I see happening around me or what the circumstances are. I know that God is moving on my behalf and arranging things in my favor and for my benefit.

In the face of difficulties, does it matter what we think and what we say? Absolutely. By now I hope you are convinced of that. Maintaining a daily positive expectation is beneficial every day of your life, but especially as you do the work to conquer your limiting beliefs. The result is that we maintain hope in our future. Without hope, it will be almost impossible to master your mindset.

Proverbs 13:12 (NIV) "Hope deferred makes the heart sick, but a longing fulfilled is a tree of life." Don't lose your hope.

#13. Face and overcome resistance.

Why is changing our mindset often so difficult? If you are following this process and doing the work, but you are still struggling, be encouraged, as you are likely meeting your resistance. Resistance is one of the most certain forces to rise up against you just as you attempt to do something worthwhile, creative, healing, spiritual or simply positive in your life. Expect it to come especially if the work you are attempting to finish has purpose and significance attached to it. Don't be surprised when it comes as you are conquering your limiting beliefs!

Resistance reveals itself in many forms. No matter the source, it is your enemy. It can be your own flesh and bad habits that hold you back or it may be the enemy of your soul. Sometimes, it can even be friends, family, coworkers, or a stranger that resistance uses to derail us, deny us progress, discourage us, or otherwise stymie our efforts. The enemy is not the person it comes from, but rather the spirit behind it.

I can tell you that it seems every time I sat down to finish this book, something called for my attention - urgently. Children, business, husband, friends, emails, sleep, hunger or any other distraction that could keep me from working in my purpose. Most people who have written a book will tell you it wasn't the writing that was hard, it was finding the time to actually write.

The book, *The War of Art*,[3] by Steven Pressfield is a simple but profound read and talks about resistance in its most naked form. The author says, "Resistance is the most toxic force on the planet. It is the root of more unhappiness....To yield to resistance deforms our spirit. It stunts us and makes us less than we are and were born to be. If you believe in God...you must declare resistance evil, for it prevents us from achieving the life God intended when He endowed each of us with our own unique genius."

Steven Pressfield goes on in the book to give many descriptive qualities of our enemy. He says that resistance is: invisible, internal, insidious, implacable, impersonal, infallible, fueled by fear, universal, never sleeps, plays for keeps, only opposes in one direction, most powerful at the finish line, and recruits allies.

Resistance is truly our enemy, the enemy to our purpose. We have to push through the distraction of resistance, speak truth to its lies, and understand that we are usually attacked in the area of our greatest gifting, in the pursuit of our creating something that is part of our divine destiny. The world needs what we uniquely can offer, and resistance wants to ensure our work never sees the light of day. In my life, I have found that the attack of resistance comes most intensely in the areas which I now recognize as my calling.

Expect resistance. See it in yourself and in your surroundings. Acknowledging it will strip it of some of its power. Using its presence to further underscore that what you are trying to do is necessary and important work for your soul will eventually render its attack unfruitful. Push onward, defy and beat resistance. Don't quit even in the face of failure. Nothing worth doing will happen without resistance.

#14. Repeat and reuse.

Respect the process, you'll get better at it every time. You will need to do this again and again in your life because the battle against limiting beliefs will be with us as long as we are breathing. You will find over time that you are victorious more quickly in some areas, while others seem to take longer to overcome and change.

Perhaps there are some additional steps you need to add to this method for your situation. Adapt it and build on it, but know that you will always be in a battle for your mind, and eliminating limiting beliefs is the only way you can truly start to pursue your purpose.

✠

MINDSET SHIFTS

1. What patterns in your family would you like to see change? Identify what you believe has been a generational cycle and commit to breaking that recurring stronghold in your family using the method in this chapter.

2. Resistance shows up in many forms in our lives, especially as we are attempting to do something purposeful. Meditate on the last time you faced resistance. Was the form of it something that recurs often for you? If so, develop strategies to recognize and overcome resistance in that area of your life.

3. 2 Peter 1:3-11 gives us seven aspects of God's divine nature to supplement our faith, our positive mindset. How would you rate yourself in these areas? Consider how you can improve with a goal for each one:

1.Moral excellence:

_____

2. Knowledge:

_____

3. Self-control:

_____

4. Patient endurance:

_____

5. Godliness:

_____

6. Brotherly affection:

_____

7. Love for everyone:

_____

4. Implement the fourteen-step process in this chapter to a specific limiting belief you are struggling with.

THE PROCESS TO CONQUER LIMITING BELIEFS

(1) Where are you? Weary, wounded, or wrecked?

(2) Who told you that?

(3) What has it cost you? What will it cost you in the future?

(4) Decide: enough is enough!

(5) Visualize how your life will change if you overcome this limiting belief.

(6) Ask for and extend forgiveness and open your spirit to God daily.

(7) Consciously control your thoughts.

(8) Watch your input and output.

(9) Replace your negative statements and thoughts.

(10) Choose love, express emotions, and develop nurturing relationships.

(11) Practice daily prayer and meditation (First 30/Last 30 rule).

(12) Maintain a daily positive expectation.

(13) Face and overcome resistance.

(14) Repeat and reuse.

CHANGE YOUR PERSPECTIVE

When you are struggling, sometimes you just need a different perspective.

Read it from top to bottom.

Today was the absolute worst day ever
And don't try to convince me that
There's something good in every day
Because, when you take a closer look,
This world is a pretty evil place.
Even if
Some goodness does shine through once in a while
Satisfaction and happiness don't last.
And it's not true that
It's all in the mind and heart
Because
True happiness can be attained
Only if one's surroundings are good
It's not true that good exists
I'm sure you can agree that
The reality
Creates
My attitude
It's all beyond my control
And you'll never in a million years hear me say
Today was a very good day

Now read it from bottom to top and notice how everything changes.

This poem was written in 2014 by New York teenager Chanie Gorkin.

CHAPTER FIVE
Pursuing Purpose

If you want to find your purpose in life,

find your wound.

– Pastor Rick Warren

She did not consider her destiny;

therefore her collapse was awesome.

– Lamentations 1:9 (NKJV)

Pursuing Purpose

$\mathcal{M}$ astering our mindset and conquering limiting beliefs is an ongoing worthwhile endeavor, allowing us to continuously clear away the obstacles that stand between us and our destiny. It is simply impossible for us to understand and operate in our purpose if we are held back by the thoughts that want to keep us small.

My hope is that you have learned at this point in the book to identify your limiting beliefs and take yourself through a process of eliminating them. You will engage in this work for the rest of your life, but now that you have the ability to do so, we can move from mastering mindset to pursuing purpose.

I believe that all of us are born with an innate desire to find out why we exist and what is the purpose of our presence on earth. Belief in an intentional, specific Creator makes this search even more necessary because not doing so would negate the idea that each of us has unique, purposeful value.

The mistake that many make, however, is to see the act of pursuing purpose as this intense, existential exercise that must result in a profound, larger-than-life conclusion. It seems many will avoid the pursuit altogether because they feel that unless they were sent to this earth to cure cancer or broker world peace, then purpose becomes a flat, empty word.

Instead, I challenge you to see purpose in the seemingly trivial aspects of life, not only in what is outwardly consequential. If we can distill life's purpose down to one goal, I submit that goal is simply to change someone's life for the better. The Webster's definition of purpose is "the reason for which something is done or created or for which something exists".

If you were to interview both the well-known contributors of meaningful change in this world along with the unknown souls who were successful in walking out their purpose in their smaller circle of influence, I believe they would have the same evaluation of their time on earth. What would stand out to them, in retrospect, are the lives they impacted and improved. All of their accomplishments, small and large, would ultimately point to the same sentiment in the end.

Let's move forward in this discussion with the idea that the reason you were created is to change someone's life for the better. The pursuit of purpose then becomes a need to answer the question of "How? In what way will I uniquely and positively impact the lives over which I am given influence?"

In his book, *In Pursuit of Purpose*,[1] Dr. Myles Munroe defines purpose as "the original intent in the mind of the creator that motivated him to create a particular item. It is the *why* that explains the *reason* for existence."

He goes on to say, "Every product is produced by purpose for a purpose. It exists for its original purpose and thus can find its true fulfillment only in performing the purpose for which it was created. Until purpose is discovered, existence has no meaning."

The meaning of life is to find your gift.

The purpose of life is to give it away.

– Pablo Picasso

Pursuing purpose on your path to destiny begins with understanding the gifts that have been placed uniquely inside of you and developing the talents needed to put those gifts into action. It is important to make the following distinction:

We are born with gifts.
We develop talents.
We pursue purpose.
We are guided by genius.
We experience destiny.

Gifts are the natural abilities placed inside of you as you were formed in your mother's womb. They are the things in life you do best with the least amount of effort. Gifts are inherently what make each of us completely different and special, and what creates a world of such diversity and intrigue. You cannot create gifts in yourself, they either exist or they do not.

It is possible, however, not to use or develop a gift. The mere fact that you were endowed with a special gift is not enough to bring you to your purpose. You must begin to work with that gift, explore it, understand it, and mature it.

The greatest athletes in this world were not at the top of their game as children. They were obviously given a specific gift and aptitude to excel in their sport, but without identifying that gift, painstakingly working on it and pushing themselves, they would have never risen to the top of their field. The expert in anything was once a beginner.

This is where talent comes into the picture. A talent is an aptitude or skill. Take a gift, which is the raw material, apply time and effort, and you develop a talent. Talents grow as you invest in them. Talent is the willful application of a gift combined with the sacrifice of effort and endurance. It is talent which is noticed and rewarded, not a gift. It is sad to consider how many people "die with their music in them" because they never stepped out to develop their gift into a talent and offer it to the world.

Our gifts, combined with the emergence of talent, point us to our purpose. This chapter is about pursuing your purpose and helping you define it. Pursuing purpose is a continual, ongoing process which alters and broadens as we work on our talents and our influence is increased.

Pursuing purpose is a path, but not a straight line. It is

something you do, a learning experience, a tapestry of unique successes and failures which create the picture of your destiny. We experience destiny as a result of pursuing purpose.

We don't set out to create or pursue our destiny. *Purpose* is what we pursue; destiny has no definition without living out our purpose. In fact, it is often at the end of a life that destiny becomes clear and hopefully fulfilled. The desire of my heart is to fulfill my destiny on earth, and I wish for you the same.

All throughout this process of pursuing purpose, genius comes alongside to guide us. What is genius? In the Roman religion, the Latin word *genius* was defined as the individual instance of a general divine nature that is present in every individual person, place, or thing.

It's interesting now in our culture that we define genius as "exceptional intellectual or creative power or other natural ability." We call people geniuses, or we say, "that idea is genius." It is a recognition of something special or set-apart.

The Roman religion was polytheistic and believed inanimate objects could have spiritual qualities. The Christian faith today believes in the Trinity and the indwelling of the Holy Spirit in a child of God. The Romans were partially right, there is genius inside of us, but I believe that is defined as the Holy Spirit of God, guiding and encouraging us in our pursuit of purpose.

Each of us is a unique creation of our Heavenly Father.
No two of us are completely alike. No one else has
exactly the same gifts and talents that we have been
given. We should increase those talents and gifts and
use them to leverage our uniqueness.

— James E. Faust

God endowed you with gifts and has given you a purpose, something to do in this life, something only you can do. Before you were born, God wired you with certain ambitions, desires, and a drive to play a particular role in history. A role that only you can play. And because your giftings are so unique, and your purpose so specific, your destiny is truly your own and no one else's.

If no two snowflakes are the same, no two fingerprints alike, you can be sure that you are created by an intentional God who put inside of you specifically what you need to carry out your purpose and experience your destiny. Ephesians 2:10 (NLT) says, "For we are God's masterpiece. He has created us anew in Christ Jesus, so we can do the good things He planned for us long ago."

Some of us know our gifts, others do not. How do you discover the gifts God has put inside of you if you are not sure? I will not attempt to present any exhaustive guide to finding your gifts as there are many professionals in the world who thrive in this niche and so many resources available to you to help you in this area. There are books to read, personality and gifting tests to take, and many experts to listen to.

What I can tell you is that there are a few quick clues that may help you understand your natural gifts. Ask yourself:

- What unique qualities draw people to me?
- In what area are people constantly asking me for advice?
- What comes easy to me but not to others?
- Look at your family - what gifts may be inherited?
- In what area of life have I experienced my biggest trials?
- What books are on my bedside table?
- What do I imagine doing repeatedly and happily? (even for free!)

Sometimes discovering your gifts can be a painful process. Consider that often your most meaningful gift, your core gift, is harder for you to verbalize. Fear may keep you from seeing your most profound gifting. Why? Often the fear arises from your confusion regarding what to do with your gift.

Your core gift is your deepest passion, deepest feeling, and where you want to express your most authentic self. But that is often where you incur the greatest wounding, so you may naturally spend a lot of time fleeing that gift. You remember the pain, shame, and embarrassment you've been made to feel around that vulnerable part of yourself. You don't want to feel that way again, so you avoid your core gift. But the sense of having missed it in your life, the lack of purpose, hounds you as you know deep inside you were meant for greater things.

For many years I would "package" myself for other people. I

learned that my type-A personality, outspokenness and physical presence as a strong woman in the corporate world often made others feel uncomfortable. I quickly learned to hold myself back and not embrace my gifts solely for the purpose of allowing others to feel OK about themselves.

This became second-nature, especially around other women, until my husband pointed it out to me one day. He asked me why I was always "dumbing myself down" in certain scenarios, especially in group settings. I soon realized that the harsh judgments I had received from others in the past (when I was operating in my gifts) made me shrink back and literally shut up.

Once I had this revelation, I was determined never to do it again. I committed to be my authentic self in all settings, and to reject other's limiting judgments. I vowed to examine my actions and words, and if they stemmed from my sense of self, my integrity, my values and my good intentions, then any issue someone had with me was their problem, not mine. What a freeing feeling! Ever since that breakthrough, my purpose began to unfold and my understanding of my giftings became so much clearer.

I love this poem from Marianne Williamson's book, *Return to Love*:[2]

> *Our deepest fear is not that we are inadequate.*
> *Our deepest fear is that we are powerful beyond measure.*
> *It is our light, not our darkness*
> *That most frightens us.*

We ask ourselves

Who am I to be brilliant, gorgeous, talented, fabulous?

Actually, who are you not to be?

You are a child of God.

Your playing small

Does not serve the world.

There's nothing enlightened about shrinking

So that other people won't feel insecure around you.

We are all meant to shine,

As children do.

We were born to make manifest

The glory of God that is within us.

It's not just in some of us;

It's in everyone.

And as we let our own light shine,

We unconsciously give other people permission to do the same.

As we're liberated from our own fear,

Our presence automatically liberates others.

The more you use your gifts, the stronger they become. Exercising your gifts is the essence of living. When you are determined to pursue your purpose, not only will the world make room for you, but it will also pay you for your gifts! Proverbs 18:16 (NKJV) says, "A man's gift makes room for him, and brings him before great men." Gifts open doors of opportunity.

The true American dream not only provides the freedom to use your gifts and talents to achieve your highest goal but also gives you the freedom to fulfill your purpose in life. You are meant to work in ways that suit you, drawing on your natural talents and gifts. This work, when you find it and commit to it, is the key to happiness.

— Dennis Kimbro

Have you ever stopped to consider whether or not your chosen career fits with the way you were designed? Are you intentional about the choices you are making, or are you simply doing what others expect of you? Are you chasing wealth instead of pursuing purpose?

How do you know if you are pursuing your purpose? Remember in identifying limiting beliefs, our feelings are a strong indication of where we are. Do you feel like you are betraying your real self? Is your spirit enhanced, or drained? Does it seem you are compromising who you are? This chapter is meant to facilitate the defining of purpose in your life.

In order to help you discover, validate or explore your purpose, I use a Purpose Venn Diagram. A Venn diagram is an illustration of the relationships between and among sets or groups of objects that share something in common by depicting intersections.

A version of this particular diagram has been floating around on social media for several years. I could not find the original source of it, nor did anyone claim its creation. What I found was a strong starting point, but I implemented many changes and added my own concepts. Overall, I made every label start with a "P"... mainly because I like alliteration but also in hopes it will make you remember the information more easily.

You may go through this exercise many times in your life, or you may use it once to discover your highest purpose. You can also use it to help you understand how the different activities of your life fit together or to prove that what you are doing right now is the correct path. In any case, it is a tool that you can leverage time and time again to make career and personal choices, a tool that offers clarity and understanding of how to better use the gifts God has given you. I have also used this diagram to assist people with new business ideas to prove or disprove their validity.

The base version of the Purpose Diagram shows the intersection of four circles: Passion, Proficiency, Pertinence, and Profit.

The circles represent the following:

Passion - Everything that you are passionate about
Proficiency - Everything that you are great at
Pertinence - Everything that the world needs
Profit - Everything that you would be paid to do

Where all of the four circles intersect, we find **Purpose**.

```
                        PASSION


  PROFICIENCY      ●         PERTINENCE


                  PROFIT
                                ●  PURPOSE
```

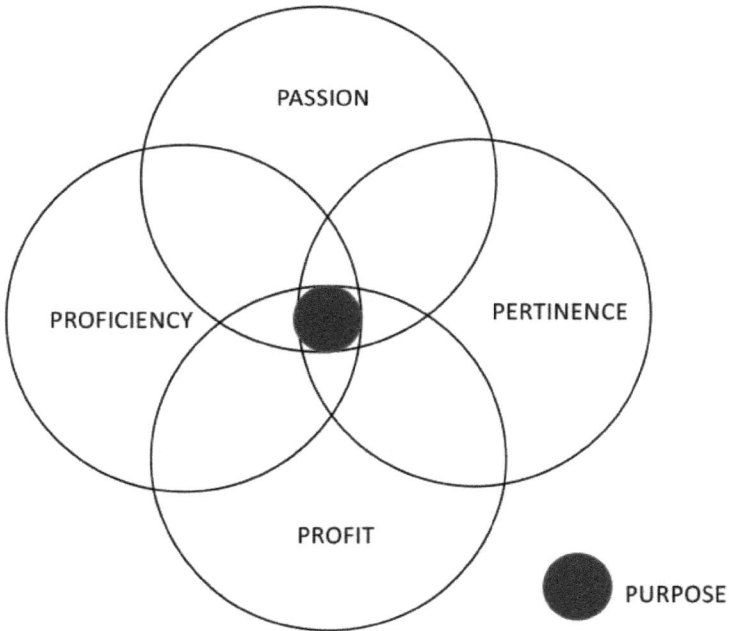

Let's examine this in more detail. **Passion** is an indicator of what matters to you and things that you truly enjoy doing. As part of purpose, it is critical that we feel passionate about what we are pursuing. You may have passions stronger than those that land in your purpose circle, and there is a place for them in your life as we will discuss later. But in order for something to qualify as purpose, a level of passion must exist. This is what will keep you going through the difficulties, doubts, and failures that are sure to exist in any worthwhile endeavor.

Proficiency means you are good at something. There are many things in the world that you are good at. Skills that you have honed, talents that you have developed and just things that come easily to you. While not all pursuits at which you excel qualify for purpose, it is crucial that you are good at that thing which you define as purpose in your life, or there will be no fruit from your labors. Purpose makes competence necessary; without it, we really don't need to be excellent at anything.

Pertinence is defined as something the world needs or wants. That circle represents everything that the world has need for...it is truly a huge circle. The point of including it as part of purpose, however, is to underscore that if you are not filling a need, you are not possibly in your purpose. This is the core of entrepreneurism as well: find a need and fill it. If you fill all the other three categories (passion, proficient, profit), but there is no need for what you offer, this cannot be defined a life's calling as you have little chance to impact anyone's life for the better.

Profit is the term most relatable to entrepreneurs, but to everyone else, it is defined as all the things in the world you can get paid for doing. Common sense says that not everything you can make money at can be defined as purpose, but purpose must come with provision. God did not design us to walk in lack as we pursue purpose. Yes, there will be times of financial challenges, but eventually true purpose will bring with it provision. The amount is not important, but walking in purpose means you will always have what you need.

Previous students have challenged the profit or provision aspect of defining purpose by using examples of those in ministry or charitable occupations who appear to have little possessions in life. I have met enough of these people to understand that even though financial challenges come and go (as they do for all of us), the experiences always build their faith and never did God not reward that faith with provision. Somehow it always works out.

How about someone like Mother Teresa? Her work was beyond admirable and she lived a life amongst the poorest in this world. She took a vow of poverty, but the truth is, she eventually had the vast resources of the Catholic Church at her disposal if she truly needed them. God provided for her even though she lived the simplest of lives. She was undoubtedly walking in her purpose, lacking no good thing.

At the intersection of these four circles is where you can discover **Purpose**. Purpose is something that you love to do, you are good at, the world needs, and you can make money doing. As I said earlier in this chapter, it does not always have to be something profound and worldly. At some point in their lives, many people are walking in their purpose by simply providing for their family in an occupation which fits all four circles to some degree. Purpose can morph as our lives and influences change, so don't despise the small beginnings or be discontented in well-doing.

It is when you are in your purpose that you find your greatest power, possibility, prosperity, provision, productivity, pleasure, and peace. There are four additional intersections that are worth exploring in this Purpose Venn Diagram as you can see below: Pastime, Profession, Position, and Pursuit. All of these have a place in your life at one time or another even though they don't equate to purpose.

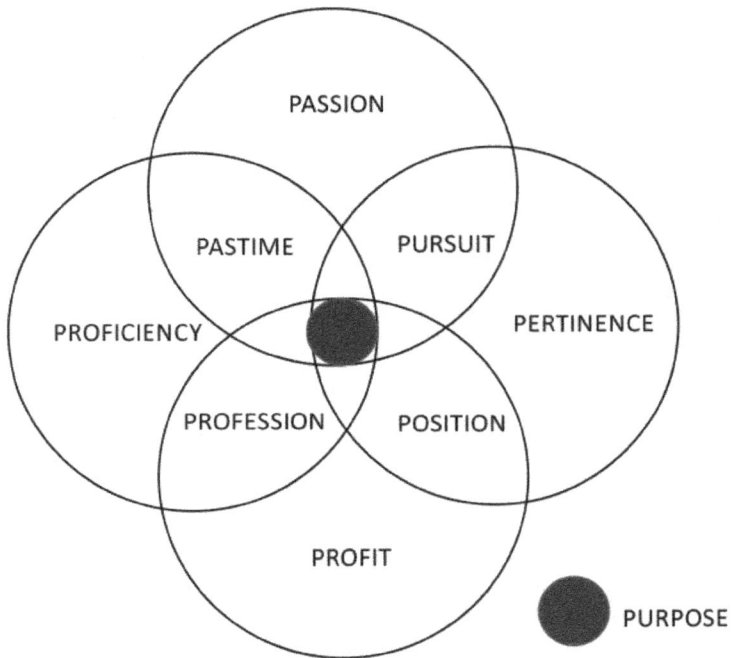

Where Passion and Proficiency intersect, you find your **Pastime.** Another term for it can be hobby or leisure-time activity. This is something that you love to do (passion) and you are very good at (proficiency). However, there is not necessarily any money to be made at this endeavor and the world doesn't really need it from you. Pastimes are important in life as an outlet for our creativity and stress relief. They are a way to use our gifts and talents that are not core to our purpose.

Profession is the intersection of Proficiency and Profit. This is where I think many people get stuck in their careers. They find themselves decades into an industry or job where they are making money, and they are good at it, but there is no passion involved and whether or not the world really needs what they do is questionable. They themselves can often feel stuck and dispensable. We have all likely found ourselves in a Profession at some point, but the danger is in staying there. There is progression in Profession, because you have a skill set that allows you to be promoted and move forward in that niche. However, the lack of Passion becomes more and more of an issue as time passes.

The intersection of Profit and Pertinence creates **Position**. This is pragmatic because you are getting paid to fill a need, but it is not crucial that you are particularly good at it, nor do you likely have any lasting passion for the work. Position is a necessary step in our work lives. You can equate this to a young person's first job or a time in someone's life where they just needed to generate extra income. There is no progression in Position, because generally you aren't developing a deep skill set, and the lack of passion tends to make that work temporary. Many move from Position to Profession...and hopefully onto pursuing Passion thereafter.

Pursuit is where Pertinence and Passion intersect. You have found something that matters to the world and a need you can meet, and you just so happen to be passionate about it as well. Pursuit can be equated to a philanthropic mission in your life. Often this is something that is borne out of charity work or socially-conscious efforts to address world problems. If you love going to

Africa with your church missions team to dig wells for fresh water provision, this is a Pursuit. It is a worthy and needed activity, and you care deeply about it. Clearly there is no Profit possibility for you, nor do you need to be worried if you are particularly Proficient in the work at hand.

We need Pursuits and Pastimes in order to live a fulfilling life and give back to our fellow man. We are blessed when we use our Passion and time in this manner, and it makes us healthier individuals. Professions and Positions should mostly be transitory in our lives, meaning that we pass through those stages at necessary times. Purpose is a process. Working our way through Positions and Professions helps us to learn more about who we are, what we have to offer, and how we can find the intersection of Purpose in our lives.

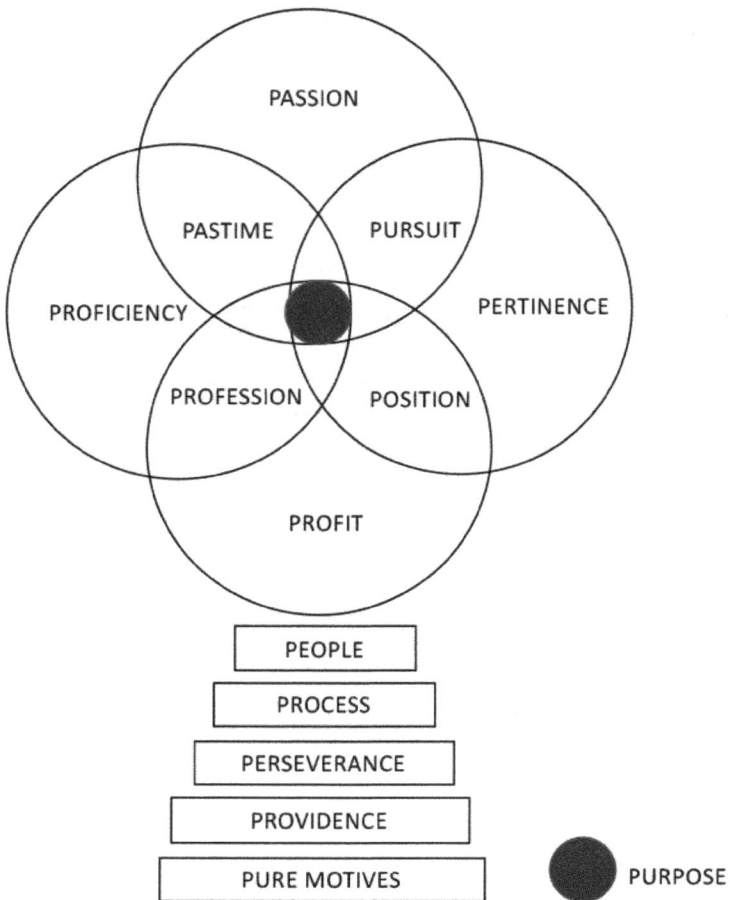

Using this Venn diagram to help define Purpose or understand where you are right now in your Pursuit should be an illuminating exercise for you. As I thought more about the use of this tool, however, I began to see that there were some general guidelines missing. I want this effort to be productive for your soul and for you to have the right mindset about pursuing Purpose, so I added five **Pillars** to the diagram:

> People
> Process
> Perseverance
> Providence
> Pure Motives

You must surround yourself with the right **People** on your road to Purpose. You were not made to go it alone in this world. As I discuss in the next chapter, we all need to have mentors, counselors, and people of faith who can speak into our lives and help us make the right choices from a place of wisdom and experience. It is not possible to figure this all out on your own.

Other viewpoints or assessments of your gifts and talents will help you craft what purpose looks like for you. It is typical for us not to see our strengths and weaknesses correctly, so find those trusted voices who can take off your blinders. Remember that you also need the purposes of others in order to fulfill your own purpose.

I cannot mention often enough that Purpose is a **Process**. This is not about arriving, but a continual journey that helps us focus and define what our purpose looks like as our talents mature and our experience grows. I don't expect to feel the same way in two years as I do today regarding my gifts and how I am using them to better the world. I know that everything I do is a feedback loop that will help me continue to grow.

Young people especially need to understand the importance of

Process so that they do not become impatient with the way Purpose unfolds. Each person's process looks different, but it just doesn't happen overnight and often there can be pain and frustration in the midst.

Embrace all of it and keep pushing forward, meaning you must have **Perseverance**. The Calvin Coolidge quote at the end of this chapter used to hang in my dad's office and I've looked at it hundreds of times as a child. The reminder to "Press On" cannot be said enough, as nothing worth achieving comes without a price.

There is no shortcut to Purpose, nor would you really want there to be. Something deep happens through your Perseverance, through not quitting, and through the bumps and bruises you sustain along the journey. A depth of character develops which adds authority to your Purpose and draws people to you. It is through this where influence grows, as discussed in the next chapter.

Only God knows the purpose for your life.

– Dr. Myles Munroe

Providence means having God involved in each step of the journey. Pursuing Purpose without His influence or guidance seems unwise at best. After all, your Creator would be best able to reveal what He has placed inside of you and why. Can a created being know its Purpose without the involvement of its creator?

In the story of Job, God made it clear to him that he could not possibly understand God's ways without knowing His purposes.

Job needed God to answer all of the "why" questions, just like we do, because Job clearly had no answers himself. We don't get all of the answers immediately, and some remain a mystery, but God is the source we should be asking.

Job 38:2-4, 6-7, 18, (NLT) says, "Who is this that questions my wisdom with such ignorant words? Brace yourself like a man, because I have some questions for you, and you must answer them. Where were you when I laid the foundations of the earth? Tell me, if you know so much...What supports its foundations, and who laid its cornerstone as the morning stars sang together and all the angels shouted for joy? Do you realize the extent of the earth? Tell me about it if you know!"

This challenge to Job from God goes on and on. Only God could answer these questions, and only He can truly reveal to you His purpose in creating you. But know that you were created on purpose, with a specific purpose. Your job is to discover it with His help.

All the ways of a man are clean and innocent in his own eyes (and he may see nothing wrong with his actions), but the Lord weighs and examines the motives and intents (of the heart and knows the truth).

– Proverbs 16:2 (AMP)

My fifth and final pillar on which the pursuit of Purpose rests is **Pure Motives**. Simply fulfilling all four circles at once is not enough to define purpose, at least not a purpose which is inherently good and moral. We also must check our motives and ensure that they are pure. Otherwise, purpose can become a tool for our gain only.

A good example of this is Bernie Madoff, the infamous Ponzi scheme villain. He clearly found the intersection of all four circles in his life: he was passionate about making money, he was very good at it, there was profit to be made, and the world thought they needed what he was offering. People literally begged him to let them invest in his fake funds.

On paper and through examining the Venn diagram, it seems to be the obvious realization of purpose. But in the end, Bernie Madoff lacked pure motives. That is an understatement of course; actually, he was a narcissistic manipulator who was willing to hurt anyone, even his own family, as he lied and cheated his way into stealing people's fortunes.

He not only destroyed his life, but so many people around him paid a high price for such a twisted pursuit of purpose. Any purpose based on greed or impure motives will eventually collapse and there will always be collateral damage to those closest to you.

I'm not suggesting that all people pursuing Purpose without pure motives have diabolical plans in mind, but there are many who do so with the wrong motivation. Not a motivation to hurt others, but one borne out of their own pain and driven by unhealthy and limiting beliefs. Such misguided motivation will ultimately prevent their purpose from positively impacting the world.

In *The Purpose Driven Life*,[3] Rick Warren said that moving from success to significance involves changing what drives your life. Are you driven by guilt, the approval of others, by greed, by fear, by resentment, by insecurity, by the past, by your parents or are you driven by a pure desire to experience the satisfaction of discovering your purpose and living your destiny? Examine your motives and heal those that are based in toxic beliefs. Go back to the process in Chapter 4 to do so.

The purpose of life is not to be happy. It is to be useful, to be honorable, to be compassionate, to have it make some difference that you have lived and lived well.

— *Ralph Waldo Emerson*

Is it worth doing all of this to pursue purpose? Perhaps we just need to move through our lives the best we can and find satisfaction in what we've been given, while doing everything to the best of our ability. Of course, we should always strive for contentment in our lives. Is the word "purpose" a moral weight? Does pursuing it seem impossible and out of reach?

I've read articles from thought leaders that argued pursuing purpose is simply an exhausting stumble down a path of disappointment for many people. Will everyone take up the challenge? No, certainly not. Is everyone meant to find their purpose? I believe so, but as I stated in the beginning of this chapter your purpose itself does not have to be profound on a global scale to matter; in reality, it is profound just to improve the life of one person while you are here. That is worthy of the pursuit in itself.

I encourage you not to get caught up in the idea that purpose only matters if it is deemed "big" and "significant" by the world's standards. Seek instead to have a higher understanding of what purpose really means. It exists miraculously in the small things in life that continually confirm someone in this world needs you, your contribution, your passion, and your presence in a way that no one else can provide. Purpose fuels our existence. Keep reaching for it, we need you!

✝

MINDSET SHIFTS

1. Do you have a sense of your giftings? If so, write them down. If not, take inventory of your life and consider what you are drawn to and how people are drawn to you. What is it that motivates you? What do you dream about? What comes easily to you that you can do repeatedly with great joy? Ask family and trusted friends what gifts they see in you. Seek out resources (books, personality tests, assessments, etc.) to help you understand yourself better and identify those gifts that have been placed inside of you. Remember we all are created with unique gifts.

2. How are you actively developing your core gifts? How would you measure your talent level related to them today? What could you do in the next 90 days to deepen your talent?

3. Work through the Purpose Venn Diagram. Apply it to things you love to do, your current career, your business idea, your hobby, etc.

4. Identify times in your life where you were in Position and Profession. Are you still there today? How can you grow from those places towards Purpose?

5. Can you define your Purpose? Write it out as you understand it today. Write down what you know and what you don't know (for example, you may feel a calling to a specific career, you know what talents you must develop, but you don't know how God will get you there).

PERSISTENCE

Nothing in the world can take the place of persistence.
Talent will not; nothing is more common than
unsuccessful men with talent.
Genius will not; unrewarded genius is almost a proverb.
Education will not; the world is full of educated derelicts.
Persistence and determination alone are omnipotent.
The slogan "Press On" has solved and will
always solve the problems of the human race.

- President Calvin Coolidge

CHAPTER SIX
Understanding Influence

The American Dream is not that every man must be level with every other man. The American Dream is that every man must be free to become whatever God intends he should become.

– President Ronald Reagan

But we will not boast of things without our measure, but according to the measure of the rule which God hath distributed to us, a measure to reach even unto you.

– 2 Corinthians 10:13 (KJV)

Understanding Influence

As you progress through this book, my hope is that you are seeing the connection between conquering your limiting beliefs and the ability to pursue your purpose. The former must come before the latter, and the cycle continues throughout your lifetime.

Pursuing your purpose is a process as discussed in the last chapter, and with it we are meant to experience an increasing measure of influence within the areas of our gifting and calling. Think of influence as the filter, the funnel, or the scope that puts your purpose into focus.

Just like any brand or product in the marketplace which has its target market and followers, God did not make us to be called to everyone and anyone. He has a way of maturing us in our purpose while allowing our influence to grow at the same time.

It is very exciting when you uncover purpose, and it becomes more defined in your life, but be cautioned that you do not run ahead of that revelation and assume that the world is your audience and everyone needs to benefit from your purpose right now. It takes time, it takes refining your skills, and it takes maturity in your gifts to widen your reach and serve more people. That is the goal of influence - not only to benefit you but to reach more people and make a bigger impact on the world.

An increase in favor for influence is a mark of His blessing.

− Bill Johnson

How do we understand our influence? How is it tied to our gifting, talents, and purpose? There is a word in the Bible that is used in only one scripture, but it has such powerful revelation for us in this study: metron. Metron is a Greek word, Strong's[1] 3358, and defined as a measure, literally or figuratively, by implication a limited portion (degree).

When Paul was writing to the Corinthians, he guided them about understanding this very subject. 2 Corinthians 10:13 (KJV) says, "But we will not boast of things without our **measure**, but according to the **measure** of the rule which God hath distributed to us, a **measure** to reach even unto you."

Measure in this passage is the Strong's 3358, metron. What Paul is saying is that we do not boast of things outside of our influence or limited portion, but that we operate within what God has granted to us.

This scripture speaks to the influence over others God gives us but also encourages us to operate within the degree and measure of gifts and talents He has given each of us. There are many people who take jobs in industries they are not suited for just because that's what their father did or that's where they think they can make the most money. Choosing careers based on money or tradition with no thought to the measure of unique gifting given to you by God is certainly a recipe for life-long unhappiness and lack of fulfillment.

My business coach, Sandi Krakowski, says in her article, *Finding Our Metron*,[2] "Unfortunately we're not even asked what we love anymore as youngsters. Teachers spend more time keeping classrooms quiet while students fill out the blanks in the workbooks than they do creating the next generation of innovators and geniuses. We have lost that idea of finding our God-given talent and then empowering the next generation to do the same, preferably early on."

I know so many wonderful teachers, and they struggle with the systems and requirements that have cropped up around them from our education system. They are often stymied in their efforts to ensure students develop individually, while they are forced to meet benchmarks and enforce standards across the board.

School in our country has become a cookie-cutter factory to a large degree. We expect students to try to achieve their best across every subject, without thought for their natural inclinations or giftings. Yes, basic skills in English, math, history, etc. must be developed, but where is the young child allowed to find his or her natural bent? How are we helping them develop it?

Children spend 12 years trying to achieve broadly so that they can get into a college which hopefully specializes in the area of their interest. But how do they know what that area is? Some do, many don't. Let's use an example. Johnny is making A's and B's in all of his classes except for math. What does the typical parent or teacher do? We intervene, we get worried, and we focus our efforts and Johnny's on his weakness, which is math.

We hire tutors, we make Johnny study more, and we try to fix the problem. Is that worthwhile? Yes, to a degree. We want well-rounded students and learning math is a life skill. But when does our focus on Johnny's weakness come at the price of his strengths? If Johnny is getting an A in biology, all parties are happy and nothing further in that subject needs to be done. Just keep doing what you are doing, Johnny.

But wait, is it possible that the "A" grade is a clue that Johnny has a particular gifting in that area? Should we be investing in that strength instead of his weaknesses? Some parents do this, but the system is really set up to focus children on improving, and therefore focusing on, their weaknesses. SAT and ACT scores reflect broad knowledge and ability and have no way to measure the brilliance of a heavily gifted student in a specific area. Colleges look at cumulative grades and scores, not so much individual gifting.

For 12 years, we tell our students they must to try to achieve across all subjects, and to a large degree we focus on helping with their weaknesses. Strengths are often taken for granted. Once they leave the primary school environment, the world immediately starts asking, "Who are you?" "What do you love to do?" "Where do you want to go with your career?" etc.

Once out of school, the world rewards people who know themselves and their giftings and are driven to achieve in that specific area. No sane person looks for a career in their weakness. Children must fit into the box created by our education system, but once they are out, they are expected to know exactly what they are going to do with their lives. Something about that is broken. That system does not give us the innovators, creators, and change agents that we need to continue to thrive as a country.

Strengthening your strengths will lead to

greater fulfillment than strengthening your weaknesses.

– Brett Blumenthal

My advice to parents of school-age children is to become an expert on your child's strengths and weaknesses. Strive to understand them deeply, watch them closely, and ask God to help you see the special gifts He put inside of them. Where they struggle, seek to understand why and decide how much effort is necessary to bring them to a place of improvement, satisfaction and eventually positive acceptance of that weakness.

Where they shine, focus on that strength. Find creative ways to deepen it and expose your children to opportunities that feed off of that ability and help them see different ways they can explore that gifting. Open their eyes to the possibilities and invest in their strengths.

We often hear rags-to-riches stories where the individual recounts his mother or father telling him as a young child, "You can be anything you want to be." People clap, get good feelings, and love to hear this. I've always paused at this statement and thought, is that really true? It sounds like a no boundaries approach to personal fulfillment and "pulling yourself up by your bootstraps", but is it an accurate statement?

I think it is misguided and untrue. We simply cannot be anything we want to be. I understand people who say this to children have the right motives, but it is misleading at best. No matter how hard I try, I will never be an Olympic ice skater. I wanted to be, so badly, but that was not my natural gifting. I also will never be a recording artist. I can't sing well enough, even though I love music.

We declare this sentiment so confidently to children, but it's not true that they can be anything they want to be. In fact, that statement implies that they were created by a distant, impersonal God who leaves it to us to find the path that we decide seems best no matter what our gifts may be.

Instead, let's tell children, "You can be anything God designed you to be." This implies a personal, specific, intentional Creator who designed us with purpose, giftings, and a natural bent meant to bless those around us as well as bless our own lives. He wants us to discover, nurture, and develop those giftings because the world needs us to walk in a specific purpose.

Saying this to children tells them that there is no ceiling above them when they are pursuing purpose and developing their God-given gifts. They can take them to the highest heights and do amazing, world-changing things with what God has put inside of them. I don't want to lie to my children and convince them that they can be anything they want to be. I want them to be people of destiny and purpose, intentional with their choices.

The Amplified version of Proverbs 22:6 says it best, "Train up a child in the way he should go (teaching him to seek God's wisdom and will for abilities and talents), even when he is old he will not depart from it." That is our job as parents and influencers - find a child's natural bent, their metron, and help him or her grow in that direction.

I believe that God created us with an intention and specific, unique, individual qualities and gifts meant to bless us and those around us. He knows us so well; He is not distant and impersonal. In fact, Jeremiah 29:11-13 (NIV) says, "For I know the plans I have for you, declares the Lord, plans to prosper you and not to harm you, plans to give you hope and a future. Then you will call on me and come and pray to me, and I will listen to you. You will seek me and find me when you seek me with all of your heart."

He has a plan for you, and He wants to share it with you. It shouldn't stay a mystery or be something we can't comprehend. God encourages us to talk to Him, to seek Him, and to discover His thoughts and plans towards us. How amazing that the God of the universe cares this much about each of us individually – it blows my mind!

Give in proportion to what you have.

Whatever you give is acceptable if you give it eagerly.

And give according to what you have, not what you don't have.

– 2 Corinthians 8:11-12 (NLT)

As influence and purpose go hand-in-hand, one grows with the other. When we discover our purpose and begin to walk in it as best we can, God then begins to grow our influence. Our metron grows as we sharpen our talents and have a broader reach with our gifting.

God does not expect or require us to give what we do not have. If we attempt to do that, we step outside of our metron, then we get into error and exasperation. Outside of our metron, our efforts are less fruitful, and our work can be frustrating. It is important to note that a metron is not how you perceive your leadership potential or sphere of influence, but metron is the influence that's present in your life now.

My friend Jessica calls this, "staying in your lane." Have you ever had that feeling of annoyance or disconnect with someone who steps out of his or her authority? I've experienced leaders who reach beyond their metron and sought to operate in a realm God clearly wasn't opening to them yet. It seems forced, it feels uncomfortable, and it is awkward to be led by someone operating outside of their metron. Rarely do you see much fruit in these situations.

This is one of the more common struggles I am seeing with young adults. To put it simply, they believe they should be somewhere in life, in their career, that they haven't earned yet. It's not that young people can't have a meteoric rise to success or be recognized as a phenom and truly contribute to society at a young age; rather, I'm talking about people who whine and complain that they aren't running the show.

I believe this is one of the reasons for the shocking rise in anxiety in our young people. They are believing a lie that they must be changing the world at a young age, and if they aren't an influencer or contributing to bettering the social consciousness then they are failing. It can also be seen as a sense of entitlement (see Chapter 1), or that they deserve recognition and advancement for just trying hard (participation trophy syndrome).

The problem with this toxic mindset is there is no sense of personal metron. They aren't concerned with the specifics of what God has designed them to do and the measure of influence that He currently has for them. They don't understand that being faithful in small things will continue to bring them more and more influence and greater rewards as they offer the world the gifts entrusted to them.

We must operate according to our own ability, according to our endowed gifting and developed talents and how we were specifically created. Your metron is not only defined by giftings and calling, but also by the receptivity of those you are currently influencing and serving. No matter how small your beginnings, understand and respect your metron, serve well, and watch your influence grow.

Do not despise these small beginnings,

for the Lord rejoices to see the work begin...

- Zechariah 4:10 (NLT)

How do you determine your metron, your current sphere of authority and influence? I was reading about finding your metron from a spiritual point of view, written by Sandy Warner who ministers to intercessors. As I read her eight points, I quickly saw in them the business side of finding your metron (or your marketplace). As a businessperson and entrepreneur coach, it jumped out at me that there are many similarities between how an individual defines metron as well as how a business does.

I have taken Sandy's eight points and altered them to show the similarities, and to help you understand that just as businesses need to have a strong sense of what they are offering to whom, we must do the same in our personal lives in order to be successful and fruitful. Additionally, we will be discussing developing your personal brand next, so thinking as a business will help you embrace the concept.

Steps to understanding your metron in life and in business:

1. Know your gifts and talents

What has God put inside of you? What is unique about you and for what do you have a natural inclination? Go back to Chapter 5 for the discussion of gifts and talents to explore this in more detail. The important point we need to grasp is that God will equip you with what you need to operate within your metron, so get clear on what He deposited inside of you.

In business, this is about understanding your unique selling proposition. What makes your product or service special and different? What do you have to offer that others do not?

2. Know to whom you are called

What group of people are you meant to influence, change, nurture, and serve? We are not called to everyone. God is specific. Look at who you are currently influencing now, no matter how small the group. What psychographics or demographics do they have in common? If you feel like your message is not reaching your audience right now, change your audience, not your message.

In business, this is defining your target market. The audience for which you have developed your product or service, the audience who is most likely to want or need what you are offering.

3. Know your assignments

Where does God want you to use your gifts and talents?

This changes as you grow and develop. Matthew 25:21 (NLT) says, "...Well done, my good and faithful servant. You have been faithful in handling this small amount, so now I will give you many more responsibilities..." God will expand the application of your gifts as you are faithful to use them.

In business, this is about understanding and then growing your market and service offering. Normally when one product or service is successful for a specific target market, additional products or services can be developed for that same audience.

4. Know your measure of faith

As you begin to move into your purpose, remember you will encounter resistance. Push through that and understand the difference between resistance and a gentle warning to change course. Faith is a muscle and it will grow when exercised. Our metron, our sphere of influence, will be no larger than our faith in what we are doing and our ability to push through resistance.

In business, this is about understanding your risk tolerance. You must have a measure of risk in order to succeed, but reaching beyond the risk you can tolerate is dangerous and unwise. As you begin to trust your decisions and your vision for your product or service becomes clearer, your risk tolerance will grow.

5. Know your pattern of successes and failures

When you are operating in your metron, you will encounter both success and failure. Sometimes the failure is more important (see the last chapter of this book), often it is more revealing than success. Take notice. Your greatest testing and failure are many times directly within the area of your greatest gifting. There is a message in that mess and a passion that develops from failure because you understand the lessons so intimately. Share your failures, let them shape you in a way that your audience will see the authority you gain from them. This is likely where your target market will be most responsive because they see you are genuine.

In business, understanding the pattern of successes and failures is what helps define your niche. Your message is more easily crafted from these experiences, and therefore your audience embraces your offering more quickly.

6. Know your opponent

Resistance to your work will come from within and from outside sources. Expect it, as I have already discussed in this book. In fact, I would argue that you are not truly operating in your metron unless you face a measure of resistance, meant to keep you from your good work.

In business, you need to know who your competitors are, and how you differentiate yourself from them. Also, who are they not? Don't try to position against everyone. Stay in your lane.

7. Know revelation

Look for signs, ask for supernatural help, and understand that nothing is a coincidence. All things you experience can be used for good. When you don't know, ask. Revelation is available to you. James 1:5 (NIV) says, "If any of you lacks wisdom, you should ask God, who gives generously to all without finding fault, and it will be given to you."

In business, you must continue to learn and expand your knowledge. Look for resources that surround you to help you grow and develop wisdom. Ask for help from those who have gone before you. Use mentors and coaches. Be willing to listen to and use constructive criticism. Don't stop learning. Your business will be better for it.

8. Know your covering

We are not made to go it alone in life. In pursuit of our purpose, we need the right people around us to stretch, support, guide and cheer us on. Who is your counsel? Choose wisely but be accountable to someone. Proverbs 15:22 (NIV) says, "Plans fail for lack of counsel, but with many advisers they succeed."

In business, there are boards of advisors for good reason. Guidance for the company growth and operations is necessary from those who have a different view and ability to see the big picture. Leaders know they do not have all the answers, and business benefits greatly from trusted counsel.

When you understand your metron, when you know how to define it and operate in it, it will begin to expand and grow as you push through resistance and as your giftings, talents, and purpose are more defined. Then your influence grows. We must allow ourselves to develop and mature in our purpose.

There is God-given favor within our metron. Remember that likability, charisma, talent, and intellect are all contributing factors, but definitely there is a bit of an "x factor" in the equation. This explains why some of the most unlikely people make the greatest impact in the world.

Growing your metron is about serving. You need to serve more people, be faithful, be teachable, stay in your lane and don't quit.

We are all broken, that's how the light gets in.

– Ernest Hemingway

Some of you reading this are feeling that you are too broken and have made too many mistakes in your life to ever have any influence. You doubt you even have unique gifts or that you could be used to help another person.

It is primarily through our brokenness and pain, however, that God uses us and molds us. Nothing is wasted. I urge you to see the hard times in your life differently, to change your mindset and stop believing the lie that your usefulness has expired or that there is nothing you have to offer.

As long as you are breathing and waking up to another day, there is purpose for your life. Begin to look at the challenges you have endured and examine how you might use those experiences to help other people. See your scars as battle trophies, as life experience that validates your purpose and defines your metron.

In the Japanese culture, the art of Kintsugi is practiced. You can read more about it at the end of this chapter, but it is centered on seeing great value in broken pottery. The scars that are visible in the ceramic piece from putting it back together is where the value lies. The lesson in this for our lives is precious.

Be yourself; Everyone else is already taken.

– Oscar Wilde

As we discuss understanding influence in this chapter, we need to continue to strive to identify our uniqueness as it affects and plays into our metron and our measure of influence.

One method for doing this work is to craft a personal brand. We are surrounded by commercial brands, whether we realize it or not. What is a commercial brand? As a company, your brand is your promise to your customers. It should distinguish you in a crowded marketplace and effectively communicate what can be expected from your product or service. Brands that are successful are consistent, easily recognized, unique, and deliver on their promise.

What is a personal brand? It is essentially the ongoing process of establishing a prescribed image or impression in the mind of others about yourself in order to express and communicate your skills, personality, and values. Who are you? What do you have to offer? Your personal brand statement should serve as inspiration and guidance for decisions you make, relationships you form, commitments you agree to, and goals you set.

As Coach Dave Buck says, "Your brand is a gateway to your true work. You know you are here to do something—to create something or help others in some way. The question is, how can you set up your life and work so that you can do it? The answer lies in your brand. When you create a compelling brand, you attract people who want the promise of your brand – which you deliver."

You can use some of the same steps and methods companies use to create your personal brand. Essentially, you are looking to find the right words which describe the essence of what you offer in a way that is compelling to your audience. This exercise is very beneficial for you to focus on who you are, where you are going, how God made you, what you offer to the world, and what matters in your life. This kind of work will allow you to be more authentic and confident, while helping you make choices that fit your brand purpose in life.

Below are several different questions to consider as you meditate on your personal brand. You will notice similarities, but they are written so that some speak to you more than others.

1. What three or four keywords describe your essential qualities or strengths quickly and clearly?

2. What is your essence factor, the core of who you are? "I know I am in my element when _____."

3. What is your authority factor, the knowledge that you hold and the skills that you possess? "People recognize my expertise in _____."

4. What is your superstar factor, the qualities that set you apart? (This factor is how you get things done or what you're known for.) People comment on my ability to _____."

5. What are your top values that you want people to recognize

in you consistently?

6. What adjectives do you want people to use when describing you?

7. When people interact with you, what feeling do you want to leave them with?

8. If you are a visual person, consider choosing colors and/or creating a logo that represents who you are and the promise you wish to "deliver."

Don't be afraid to "re-brand" as your experience grows and your metron does as well. Above all, stay true to yourself by consistently reviewing your brand and the way in which you emulate the uniqueness that God placed inside of you.

When you act or speak, ask yourself if you acted or spoke from within your brand or outside of it. Deliver on your brand promises and see your metron grow as a result of your brand consistency and faithfulness.

Don't be scared to present the real you to the world.

Authenticity is at the heart of success.

- Unknown

Once you have identified your brand words, you can move to the next step of developing a vision statement for yourself, or what is often called in business a "HUB: Hottest Undeniable Benefit" statement.

This can literally turn into your "elevator pitch" or what you tell people at parties when they ask you what you do. Answering that question isn't just about our career or how we make money, it is about how we are impacting our world. It is a statement of vision.

Your HUB statement is 1-2 sentences answering what you are best at (value), who you serve (audience) and how you do it uniquely. It sums up your distinctive promise of value and is like a personal tagline.

To help you get started writing your statement, use the following templates as a starting point, but don't let them constrain you.

> *I use my _____ and _____ for _____.*
>
> *Known for _____, I _____.*
> *Using _____ (key trait), I _____, by providing _____.*
> *Through my _____, I _____, when I serve _____.*

Here are two examples I found online for two different careers:

#1. Through my natural enthusiasm and my empathy for others, I inspire research and development professionals to develop innovative products in biotechnology. (Biotech Manager)

#2. Using my holistic insight and innovative Total Performance Scorecard principles, I promise to help my customers realize their financial dreams. (Financial Consultant)

The following is my HUB statement:

Through my passion for mastering mindset, I empower individuals to attain abundance and transform their world with their gifting and purpose.

Everyone can benefit from crafting a personal brand and HUB statement. Think about it as another step toward understanding why you are here, how you are different, and what impact you can have on those around you. We were created to bless others with our gifts. How are you doing that?

The best way to predict your future is to create it.

– Abraham Lincoln

Small beginnings and operating in our current metron does not mean that we do not have a greater vision for the future. In fact, as part of understanding your metron and your personal brand, it is important to have plans and ambitions to grow your influence and make your mark on the world. Our minds need to have a large goal to reach for.

Dr. Daniel Amen, neuroscientist and psychiatrist, talks about how your brain does not know the difference between visualization and actually doing something. The brain has the capacity to help us achieve a result we only visualize, because we have directed the brain to see it as a pre-determined outcome. Athletes are known to use this approach to visualize themselves winning a race and going through all the details in their mind repeatedly, to the point where when they get to the competition, it is as though the brain already knows how to get them over the finish line as the winner. We can use that same technique to imagine our possibilities.

What do you see as a limitation in your life? Visualize yourself overcoming it. What do you fear doing but know is necessary to your purpose? See yourself doing that thing over and over again successfully. What skill or talent do you think you are missing in order to succeed? Direct your brain to visualize yourself operating in that skill with ease and power. What result in your life seems unobtainable? Create the scenario, meditate on it, and visualize yourself experiencing it. Leverage the power of your mind that God gave you to see the end before you even begin.

A significant exercise that I use with my students to capture the potential in their future is to write their own introduction. Here are the instructions: Pretend you are being introduced to speak at a gathering of your target audience. It is ten years into the future, and much has happened in your life. Based on your hopes, dreams, plans, and results, what would that introduction sound like?

A good introduction should answer three questions: Why this speaker, on this subject, to this audience? Include your past and recent achievements and struggles, as well as experiences that qualify you to speak about this subject to this crowd. Write it in the third person and leave your false humility out of the equation. This introduction should reflect where you want to be in ten years.

We must understand in this exercise that we can achieve

whatever the mind conceives, so reach for big things. However, recognize that God has certain plans for you as well, and He will make a way where you never knew there was a way, so be open to your plans changing and growing beyond what you could imagine!

The following is my introduction that I am sharing with you to help you write yours. I am certain I will be changing this in two years, but I will continue to reach way beyond where I am today!

MY INTRODUCTION

Dear Ladies and Gentlemen, we are pleased to have with us today Dr. Elizabeth Nader.

She is an author, certified entrepreneur and mindset coach, experienced businesswoman, motivational speaker, and creator of the "Master Your Mindset, the Master's Way" teaching series. In addition to a successful corporate and entrepreneurial career, Elizabeth's company was recently ranked on the Inc. 5,000 Fastest Growing Companies list. She holds several business degrees as well as a Doctorate in Theology.

Dr. Nader has written five books, the current one a New York Times Bestseller. She speaks all over the world encouraging people to eliminate their toxic thoughts, discover their giftings, and walk in their destiny. Dr. Nader delivers motivation and guidance weekly to her online community of thousands seeking to live their best life.

Today we get to experience her enthusiasm for overcoming obstacles and discovering purpose. Her unwavering belief in people's potential propels her clients and students into new realms in both their personal and professional lives. Welcome, Dr. Nader!

As you can see, I have some work to do! I'm excited about the future and I welcome all that God has for me, even if the details change.

Besides the highlights that you see in the introduction, I also have a list of results I want to see in my life. Things I want to accomplish that I hold next to my heart, write down in my private journal, and visualize with intention. This book is a good example of just that...20 years before I wrote this book, my first book, I had a vision for it. Not the content, not the audience, just the idea that I would write a book that stemmed from my heart's passion and sought to help others change their life for the better.

By praying about this, writing down the intention, and hiding it in my heart, I fostered the dream. I couldn't just create it out of my willpower until God made the timing right and gave me the message that flowed onto the paper with ease. So much of what happened to me in those 20 years, both good and bad, was what made it possible to write my first book.

I invite you to write your introduction and visualize your best self ten years from now. In a couple of years, pull out that introduction and re-write it. Make a list of intentions, of results you want to see in your life. Hide them in your heart and imagine them coming to pass in your life. Keep moving the goal line, keep clarifying your focus and reaching for new heights. Achievement and significance do not come by chance, they are birthed through vision and tenacity.

✠

MINDSET SHIFTS

1. Consider what your metron is as you understand it today. What unique gifts has God placed inside of you? What does your sphere of influence look like right now? How might that grow?

2. Develop a personal brand by answering the questions posed in this chapter. Look for the repeated use of certain words and phrases that may become key to defining who you are. For those so inclined, develop a personal logo with a visual representation of your brand.

3. Think about the interactions you had and decisions you made in the past week. Were they "on-brand" for you? What changes can you make so you can more easily stay true to who you truly are?

4. Develop a HUB statement as guided in this chapter, using the branding words you came up with in #2 above.

5. Write your introduction as it would sound ten years from now. Stretch yourself and weave in goals and dreams into that introduction. Adjust it every few years and always move the goal line. Dream big.

Kintsugi 金継ぎ: The Art of Precious Scars

By Stefano Carnazzi,
translated by Francesca Clemente

By repairing broken ceramics, it's possible to give a new lease of life to pottery that becomes even more refined thanks to its "scars". The Japanese art of kintsugi teaches that broken objects are not something to hide but to display with pride.

When a bowl, teapot or precious vase falls and breaks into a thousand pieces, we throw them away angrily and regretfully. Yet there is an alternative, a Japanese practice that highlights and enhances the breaks thus adding value to the broken object. It's called kintsugi or kintsukuroi, literally golden ("kin") and repair ("tsugi").

This traditional Japanese art uses a precious metal – liquid gold, liquid silver, or lacquer dusted with powdered gold – to bring together the pieces of a broken pottery item and at the same time enhance the breaks. The technique consists in joining fragments and giving them a new, more refined aspect. Every repaired piece is unique, because of the randomness with which ceramics shatter and the irregular patterns formed that are enhanced with the use of metals.

The scars become what to exhibit

With this technique it's possible to create true and always different works of art, each with its own story and beauty, thanks to the unique cracks formed when the object breaks, as if they were wounds that leave different marks on each of us.

How many beautiful messages the kintsugi technique conveys

The kintsugi technique suggests many things. We shouldn't throw away broken objects. When an object breaks, it doesn't mean that it is no more useful. Its breakages can become valuable. We should try to repair things because sometimes in doing so we obtain more valuable objects. This is the essence of resilience. Each of us should look for a way to cope with traumatic events in a positive way, learn from negative experiences, take the best from them and convince ourselves that exactly these experiences make each person unique, precious.

CHOPSTICKS STORY

A mother took her eight-year-old son to a great concert hall, a black-tie event to hear a famous composer and pianist. The little boy became restless waiting for the concert to start so as soon as his mother visited with friends he slipped from her side and ran onto the stage. He was drawn in by the Steinway, climbed up on the stool and stared wide-eyed at the keys. He placed his little fingers in the right location and began to play chopsticks in the Lincoln Center. The roar of the crowd was hushed as hundreds of frowning faces turned his direction irritated and embarrassed, they began to scream "get him out of there, who would bring a kid that young in here, where is his mother? Somebody stop him."

Backstage, the master overheard the sounds out front and quickly put together in his mind what was happening. Hurriedly he grabbed his coat and rushed toward the stage. Without one word of announcement, he stooped over behind the boy reached around both sides of him and began to improvise a counter melody to harmonize and enhance chopsticks. As the two played together the composer kept whispering in the boy's ear ,"Keep going don't quit son, keep playing don't quit, don't stop."

So it is with us; we hammer away on a projects which seems about as significant as chopsticks in a concert hall. About the time we are ready to give up along comes a master who leans over and whispers "Now keep going, don't quit, keep on, don't stop, don't quit!"

- Unknown

CHAPTER SEVEN
Money Mindset

God does not deem you to be lucky or unlucky,

your mindset does.

— Robert Kiyosaki

And my God will meet all your needs according to

the riches of His glory in Christ Jesus.

— Philippians 4:19 (NIV)

cannot recall where I saw this statistic, but it struck me, and I never forgot it. According to a nationwide study, 72% of Americans report money is their #1 stressor. That doesn't shock me, but it does underscore the need for us all to get our money issues figured out so we can eliminate or reduce this common source of stress and begin to let money flow with our purpose. Do you think money will always be a challenge in your life? It doesn't have to be!

There are many programs in the marketplace which will help you straighten out your finances. Create a budget, pay off debt, save money for retirement, etc. This chapter is not about any of those things. First things first…how is your money mindset? All of these methods to get your finances in order are so important, but also virtually useless if you have limiting beliefs regarding money. Guess what happens to the lottery winner with a poverty mindset…yes, you've seen the story before, eventually all the money is gone. No financial plan will fix a broken mindset.

Some of the best advice I ever received about money was to start on the inside first, then work to the outside. In other words, identify, clarify and eliminate those toxic ideas you have about money that are holding you back. Replace them with a healthy, affirming money mindset and then work on the details of expenses, income, debt, savings, investing, and everything else you must do to be a good manager of the money entrusted to you. The power and the results start on the inside first, as our mindset is actually controlling our money experience just as it controls everything else in our life.

I believe God wants us to prosper and have more than enough. The Bible tells us that. So, if it is true, why do so many people struggle with money? Why aren't there more people living free of the pressure of lack? Why isn't everyone walking in abundance and provision? I believe it is due to faulty thinking and a toxic mindset regarding money. The lack of money is not a circumstance, but instead the result of a wrong mindset.

This idea may actually anger some of you. We don't really want to take ownership of our money issues; we would rather blame them on our "luck" or "lot" in life. Where we were born, where we went to school, our job opportunities, our geographical location, our intelligence, our physical limitations, our spouse…the list goes on. We believe that money issues are strictly tied to our circumstances. That allows us to be free from responsibility; instead, we play the blame game without even realizing it.

Jesus said in the Bible that the poor would always be with us (see Mark 14:7). Did He say that because He knew God designed some people to be poor? Or because it is God's will that people suffer financially? Absolutely not. I believe that God wishes for all to prosper, however that looks, but He knows that some will never overcome a poverty mindset. My friend Victoria always says, "Poor is permanent, broke is temporary." Why? It's all about mindset.

I can almost hear some of you thinking, "What about poor, third-world countries? What about America's inner cities? Is it their fault they are suffering?" No. But it is a reflection of the stronghold of poverty and prevailing limiting mindsets that have, in some cases, kept entire countries, neighborhoods, and generations in the bondage of lack. It's not your fault what chains you are born into; it IS your responsibility to do all you can through God to break free of them and let Him do the rest.

My grandparents, hard-working farmers in Iowa, were quiet, humble, God-fearing, no-nonsense, generous people who fiercely loved their family, their country, and the fruits of their labor. I adored visiting the huge farm they had because I gleaned such a strong sense of my roots there and learned the importance of hard work, as well as our dependence on God for everything we have.

I'll never forget the sign they had in the entryway to their home, the quote from Saint Augustine: "Pray as though everything depended on God. Work as though everything depended on you." This so perfectly captured their attitude about life, and I think it is a great directive for us as it relates to our finances and our money mindset. We must not play the victim when it comes to our money situation; rather, we need to do all we can to improve it, while at the same time relying on God to provide as He promises. We do our part, He does His. They must move in concert for us to see results.

Having a scarcity mindset disrespects God.

Understand that with God, abundance is always available.

– Billy Alsbrooks

One of the first steps towards developing and maintaining a healthy money mindset is to stop comparing yourself to anyone else on this subject. Money plays a very spiritual, personal, and specific role in your life. What you do to generate it, spend it, save it, invest it, or give it away is unique to you, your innate gifts, developed talents, your purpose, and your deeply held beliefs about money. Not only is comparison the thief of joy, but it is a liar - what does our purpose have to do with someone else's? We are on our own path with its own specific provision.

Perhaps you are inspired by seeing someone else's success - that's understandable. Inspiration and dreaming are different than comparison and envy; the first two are propellers, the last two are prisons. The exhausting exercise of comparison also presumes that everyone's outcomes should be the same, or there is something wrong with one of the parties being compared.

America's Declaration of Independence states that all men (and women of course) are created equal with the same inalienable rights. One of those is the pursuit of happiness. Note that it does not say the *guarantee* of happiness, but rather the *pursuit*…the ability to reach for it. It is about the individual, the opportunity to create the life he or she wants without the government standing in the way. This is the American Dream.

While we are all created with equal value, we are not created with equal gifts or born into the same situations. Our value as humans is unquestionably the same, but we are each unique in a thousand ways. Therefore, our experiences and outcomes in life are different, due to our uniqueness and of course our choices. The idea of America is to give us equal opportunity, but not equal results. The results depend on us, with God's help.

Not to get political, but one of the reasons I see the movement of socialism as misguided is because it seeks to destroy the idea and value of individualism and ignores the uniqueness of gifting and purpose. It sees everyone as deserving of equal results no matter if their efforts or talents are equal. A society based on these concepts begins to lose the creativity of ideas, the energy of entrepreneurism, and the inspiration for change. Why bother with any of this, if everyone is to be completely equal? What drives you to achieve in life if the results are the same and guaranteed for everyone?

As we operate in our purpose with a healthy money mindset, God's provision may not be the same dollar amount as it is for someone else, but it will be the provision that we specifically need…more than enough, and extra with which to bless others. It's not about a dollar amount or equality with your neighbor, it's about you, your purpose, and the right provision for your life. Once the provision shows up, we need God's wisdom for how to manage and grow it.

Simply getting more money won't solve your financial issues. Rather, money amplifies what is already good or is already bad in our lives. Therefore, it makes sense that if we want to attract more money and actually have it change us for the better, we need to work on our mindset first.

Let's agree that more money changes people...either for better or for worse. See it as this equation (I added the numerical figures to assist with the illustration):

$$Old\ You + More\ Money = New\ You$$
$$(2) \quad + \quad (3) \quad = \quad (5)$$

If we apply mathematical law, we can re-write it this way:

$$More\ money = New\ You - Old\ You$$
$$(3) \quad = \quad (5) \quad - \quad (2)$$

So how do you attract more money into your life? You subtract the old you from the new you - you change your mindset! If extra money makes a new person of you, it easily follows that making a new person of you is a step on the road to having more money. Get rid of old thinking and broken concepts about money. You change first, then the money comes...and stays.

Pride wants people to think that we paid more.

Poverty wants people to think we paid less.

Gratitude doesn't care what people think;

it only cares what God thinks!

— Pastor Robert Morris

Just like our other limiting beliefs, we often "catch" many of our toxic mindsets about money as children. Often those ideas are generational, and simply get repeated again and again without much thought. In order for us to break the cycle of limiting money mindsets, we first need to identify them and consider their roots.

As an example, many people who lived through the Great Depression developed an unhealthy (but understandable) fear of lacking money. Perhaps they lost everything in the crash of 1929, or simply got to a point of such lack over the ensuing years that they didn't know where their next job or meal would come from. This went on for almost a decade for many, so that fear became stronger and more entrenched over time.

If you track the behaviors of young adults from that era, many of them grew into adulthood very concerned about money. They were careful to never waste it and were very slow to spend it on themselves or put it at risk. In some cases, what appeared to be good money management or wisdom was actually fear operating behind the scenes. They couldn't enjoy their money because they felt it could disappear any day. While they can be applauded for not being a wasteful generation, you can also see the fear as the motivator behind their decisions.

The children of these Depression-Era adults watched the way their parents dealt with money and heard the words they used to talk about it. For those still haunted by the experience of the 1930's, the fear that they had not conquered was inevitably passed down to their children. This fear could be reflected in the desire for "safe" jobs, an obsession with finding discounts, the aversion to taking risks, the false belief that money is limited and it can all disappear, and guilt that came with spending money on personal desires.

Of course, this example does not reflect everyone from that generation, and many used the experience of the Depression to propel them into greater heights. But it is a strong illustration of how life circumstances can begin to develop toxic mindsets about money. If we do not deal with those limiting beliefs, we can unknowingly hand them down to our children who then are faced with either breaking the cycle, or instead handing it down to their children.

I must digress for a moment on the subject of discounts. I've noticed something in the past few years online and on TV that has given me pause. Listen, I am the first person to say I never pay retail price. I love shopping at a discount, and there are certainly bargains to be had everywhere. However, I noticed a trend many years ago where people would spend an inordinate amount of time clipping coupons, taking small surveys for money online, and otherwise hatching plans to save pennies here and there.

There are blogs online about where to find discounts, constant ads about making money from home, apps on your phone that will track your spending and provide you pennies here and there for that information, and of course the "Extreme Couponing" TV series showing how some people have taken saving money to an entirely new level. Seeing all of this, I began to wonder just how much time some people spend chasing the discounts. If they spent that same time figuring out how to make more money rather than save it, would their lives be different?

Those coupon shows tell stories of people buying hundreds of dollars of groceries and goods for mere pennies or dollars, all due to coupons. They take everything home and show us where they are hoarding all these items...that they didn't even need. Is this a mindset of abundance or lack? Again, I'm not judging the idea of saving money, but I caution you to check where you spend your precious, limited time - on increasing or on saving? I believe it is all tied back to deeply held beliefs.

This is why I am so passionate about people getting free in the area of money - to stop the cycle of damaging mindsets that came from negative circumstances. You may be in a family that seems to always struggle with money...imagine if you were the person who changed that for generations to come! In order to do so, you must first identify the limiting beliefs about money that have held you captive.

It's simple arithmetic.

Your income can grow only to the extent that you do.

— T. Harv Eker

At the end of this chapter is a list, not at all comprehensive, of different beliefs about money. As we did in Chapter 3, take a moment to go through this list and circle the beliefs you honestly hold. Do not hesitate, immediately circle the phrase if you have ever thought it. If there are other controlling beliefs about money in your life not listed, please add them (and email them to me!).

I find it interesting that in every class I have taught on this subject, I ask people to tell me what their parents taught them about money before we go through the list of beliefs. It never fails that almost everyone who raises their hand says things like, "Save more than you spend." "Use money wisely." "Work hard." "Live within your means." etc. If I stopped there, we could skip the rest of this teaching because it sounds like everyone inherited a great money mindset! But the truth is different; we just have to dig a little.

Once we go through the list of money beliefs, people are amazed at what they circle. Not only that, but if I asked the same people who raised their hands if they are winning with money in their lives, most would say "No". Most would admit to struggling in certain areas, but yet they claim to have been taught all the right things by their parents. By now you know children pick up more by watching than by just listening. With further exploration, my students would recall stories of seeing their parents struggle with certain specific money issues or attitudes, or in some cases tell their own story of traumatic circumstances involving money that altered their mindsets as adults.

As you read through this chapter, I urge you to be willing to be honest with yourself about the limiting beliefs you have regarding money. For some reason, more than other subjects, we tend to be defensive about our money mindset issues. Perhaps it is because unfortunately as a society we equate personal worth to our bank balance. But this isn't just about how much money you have or do not have, it is about whether or not you have a healthy mindset regarding your money, so money becomes a force for good in your life.

By reading the chapters before this one, you will have learned about the definition of mindset and how we are controlled by our deeply held beliefs. All of those concepts apply in the same fashion to our money mindset, and the toxic beliefs explain why so many repel rather than attract money in their lives.

We cannot solve our problems with the same

thinking we used when we created them.

— Albert Einstein

Unmasking your deeply held limiting beliefs about money can be accomplished by admitting to areas in your financial life that are broken, identifying the beliefs behind your struggles (use the list at the end of the chapter to help), and also by contemplating a series of questions designed to make you consciously think about how your heart truly views money. I'd like to take this opportunity to challenge some commonly held beliefs.

While portions of what I write may seem overtly political, that is not my intention. I simply want you to consider a fresh view on certain areas of your money mindset that perhaps you have never questioned before. You don't have to agree with me, but please allow me to make you think. When you do discover a toxic belief about money, run it through the process in Chapter 4 to change that belief and cancel its power over your life and your finances.

1. How do you view money?

Do you see money as evil or good? Limited or unlimited? A blessing or a curse? Yours or God's? To be hoarded or shared? A means to the end or the end goal?

Money is amoral until it is put to use. In other words, money does not contain any energy, positive or negative, in its static state. Many people incorrectly think that the Bible says that money is the root of all evil, when the verse actually says that the LOVE of money is the root of all evil (see 1 Timothy 6:10). Money itself has no moral compass; rather, the manner in which money is used is when it becomes good or evil.

If I use the money I make in my business to support my family and donate to charity, then that money has become "good". If, however, I use the same money to further an addiction or to engage in illegal activities, then that money has essentially become "evil". It is a fairly simple concept, but worth noting as many people see money as evil without even questioning that mindset. I challenge you to see money, itself, as neither good nor evil until it is put to use, so you can remove that stigma.

One of the toxic mindsets behind envy and comparison is that there is a limited supply of money in the world. Therefore, if you have more, I will have less. Money is more of a spiritual issue than people realize. While in the natural world there is an actual limit to the amount of money that circulates in our economy, spiritually there is no limit. How do I know that? Because I believe that God owns everything, and in Him everything is limitless. He is my provider, and in Him there is an endless supply of what I need. That includes money, if I see it correctly.

I have met people who have been taught by their parents that having money is a curse, that it will ruin their life. Often this isn't said so directly, but in many ways modeled to them as children. It is another form of the belief that money is evil - that it will drag you into bad relationships and bad circumstances, and it just isn't holy to have money. People who hold this belief, while they must work for money, subconsciously get rid of it as quickly as they can. Essentially, they repel money in their lives.

I believe the best way to see your relationship with money is that of a manager of someone else's assets. Is your money actually yours or God's? That certainly depends on your spiritual viewpoint. I submit to you that God owns everything, and therefore what He gives you is entrusted to you to manage. If you give a money manager $100,000 and he mismanages that sum and carelessly loses your money, you will fire him and find a new manager. You certainly won't entrust him with more of your money!

Looking at yourself as the manager of God's resources changes your attitude and approach in dealing with money. It motivates you to manage it well and grow it as best you can, all while enjoying your life and taking care of the needs God has put in your path. As we will discover in the Parable of the Talents below, God gives more to those who have proven themselves trustworthy with His possessions. This is why you need to maintain a healthy money mindset.

If you believe a resource is limited, you will tend to hoard it. If, on the other hand, you believe that sharing a resource is the best way to attract more of it in your life, then your hands will be open. Hoarding money and not focusing on the importance of giving is the surest way to experience lack in your finances. The Bible says it is better to give than receive (see Acts 20:35), and that when we give it will be given back to us in greater measure (see Luke 6:38).

While it may seem counterintuitive, one of the keys to financial success is to be generous with your money, with wisdom of course. If you examine the life of a faithful giver, you will see continued growth and rewards in their personal and financial life that outmatches their giving. God is faithful in this area and I encourage you to grab hold of the life-changing principle of sowing and reaping. The only way to reap a harvest is to plant a seed. Don't eat your seed.

Finally, you have likely heard the phrase, "He who dies with the most toys wins." While we can discuss how truly empty and depressing that notion is, it really points to the toxic mindset that money is the end goal, not a means to the end. In other words, if you are striving only to make more money in your race to "win," then you will ultimately lose. The blessing comes in seeing money as a tool, as a means to the end. To what end? As a means to bless others, live an impactful life, and walk out your purpose on earth. Money fuels all of that. But if you chase it only for itself, you will come up empty when it matters most. Money is your tool, not your goal.

2. How do you view people with more money than you?

Do you envy them? Judge their lifestyle or purchases? Question whether they should make so much money? Assume they must have selfish motives?

I believe strongly that you will never have what you criticize. Do you ever find yourself making comments about someone with more money than you? How about extremely rich people? Have you ever wondered if they needed that much money or if they made it honestly?

As an example, I've heard people talk about the large financial contracts that professional athletes have. Discussions are had about whether athletes "deserve" to make that much money, or that it is obscene the way they spend it. This often comes out of the mouths of people who are more than willing to spend $250 or more on a ticket to watch them compete.

In capitalism, the market decides the prices. It is simple supply and demand. If people were not willing to pay so much to attend these games, and advertisers not willing to pay so much to have exposure to the fans, then there would not be the immense pool of money from which to fund the large contracts. It is basic economics, and you are part of that cycle in one way or another. The same applies to Hollywood and corporations.

We have to be careful how we judge people and their lifestyles. We only know what we know - the behind the scenes is usually unavailable to us. If you see a wealthy person driving a new expensive car, do you think about how many homeless people he or she could have helped with that money? What if I told you that they just gifted millions of dollars to charity the week before they bought that car? You just don't know the truth about people's lives unless you are living them.

There are times when we can rightly judge overtly bad, unethical, or illegal money behavior. Calling what is good, good, and what is bad, bad, is OK to do. However, we often do this in judgment of other people's lifestyles without all of the information. This is where we get into error, and again I say: be careful, you will never have what you criticize.

There is usually no context for judging someone's wealth or lifestyle, and everything is relative. One man's abundance is another man's lack. We are not equal in our outcomes or results, only in our value as human beings. I challenge you to keep your eyes on yourself and stop the comparison/judgment game with money.

3. How do you view business?

Do you believe businesses are inherently good or evil? Job creators or just profit machines? Out to take advantage of you or provide a necessary product or service?

The reason this question is so important is that business is what creates the flow of money. Any size business, any type, is where the cycle of money begins. Goods and services are created, and money is exchanged. Jobs are created and salaries are paid. There is no economy without business. As you read this, you are probably either a business owner or you work for one. The majority of Americans do, unless you work for the government.

Yet, there is a stigma created by some in the political sphere and definitely in the media and entertainment world that business is evil. Big bad businesses hurt the little guy and hoard all the money. The greedy companies need to be punished and "pay their fair share". Big business is the media and Hollywood's favorite villain. It started in the 1980s with many films that depicted the greed and avarice of Wall Street, and it hasn't stopped. We are told overtly and subtly that business is the bad guy.

This became especially common in the recent recession of 2008, which was due in large part to bursting of the real estate "bubble"…the avalanche of mortgages that went into default and the banks who needed to be bailed out. All eyes were turned on the big bad banks, in some cases for good reason. But what the politicians pointing their fingers forgot to tell you was that it was them, the Congress, who forced banks through legislation to loosen their lending practices so more Americans could own homes. As a result, mortgages were very easy to obtain back then, and by many people who could not afford what they were buying. Not to oversimplify it, but it was a disaster waiting to happen. And it wasn't just the fault of the banks. Politics played a huge role.

While there certainly are businesses who cheat, don't treat their workers right, or unfairly compete, does that bad light deserve to be cast on all businesses? Do you realize that if you think your company makes too much money, you are essentially wishing yourself out of a job?

There is another mindset that sees the government as a better arbitrator of the economy and source of jobs than businesses are. This has been proven false time and time again, but still there are groups who believe it. You can understand that if someone's agenda is for the government to run everything, then they must paint business as the enemy.

Entrepreneurism is the jewel of the American economy. Small businesses collectively create more jobs than any other sector, and it is why we still thrive as a nation regardless of our economic ups and downs. It is in our best interest to continue to support a culture that sees business as positive and creates an environment where entrepreneurs can continue to bring new ideas to market and not be choked by policies and attitudes that are anti-business. (Alright, maybe that got a little political.)

If you look deep into the traditional Jewish culture, a culture that historically has produced more wealth with less people than any other, you will find a healthy conviction that business is good. They believe that the only acceptable way to achieve wealth is to attend to the needs of others and conduct yourself in an honorable fashion.

In other words, the Jewish culture sees business as providing goods or services that help our fellow man, and in return, money is exchanged. A bank who loans an individual money to start a business is providing a service which helps that individual, therefore the interest earned on the loan by the banker is good, worthy money, a sign he has done the right thing. Your wealth reflects the degree to which you are helping society. Wealth is good, business is good! We can learn much from that mindset and will talk about one interesting Jewish ceremony in a few pages.

4. How do you think God views money?

Does God think about money? Does He see wealthy people as evil? Does God think it is holy to be poor? Does He make some people struggle and allow others to have it easy financially?

Because I believe money is a spiritual force, I think God has a lot to say about it. In fact, the Bible has more scriptures on money than any other topic. Since God owns everything anyway (see Psalm 50:11-12), shouldn't we try to discover how He views money? I certainly cannot begin to comprehend or fully explain God's attitude on the subject, but there are a few key things to look at from His Word.

The Bible continuously emphasizes the wealth of the patriarchs. You see this reflected in the Jewish faith as well, where the wealth of Solomon, David, and other men from the Old Testament is celebrated. God clearly highlights the blessings in their wealth for a reason. He doesn't see them as evil or less holy because of their money.

In the Parable of the Talents (Matthew 25:14-30), Jesus tells a very instructive story about money management. In the parable, the master is leaving town and gives three of his servants a different number of talents (money) each, expecting them to manage it while he is gone.

One servant is in fear of losing it and buries the money to protect it. The other two servants invest their talents and double them. None of the servants were given the same number of talents, but each had the same opportunity to use and increase their talents. One servant did nothing with his talent, and the other two invested them and doubled their worth. The master was pleased with those two servants and gave them more to manage.

The one who was in fear and buried his talent was in trouble with the master. What little he had was taken from him and he was rebuked. It is such an interesting parable on many levels related to money, our gifts and talents, and what we do with what God gives us. You can see clearly through this story that God has an expectation that we do the most with what he has entrusted to us…and when we do, more will be given. Here is the full parable:

> For it will be like a man going on a journey, who called his servants and entrusted to them his property. To one he gave five talents, to another two, to another one, to each according to his ability. Then he went away. He who had received the five talents went at once and traded with them, and he made five talents more. So also, he who had the two talents made two talents more. But he who had received the

one talent went and dug in the ground and hid his master's money. Now after a long time the master of those servants came and settled accounts with them. And he who had received the five talents came forward, bringing five talents more, saying, 'Master, you delivered to me five talents; here, I have made five talents more.' His master said to him, 'Well done, good and faithful servant. You have been faithful over a little; I will set you over much. Enter into the joy of your master.' And he also who had the two talents came forward, saying, 'Master, you delivered to me two talents; here, I have made two talents more.' His master said to him, 'Well done, good and faithful servant. You have been faithful over a little; I will set you over much. Enter into the joy of your master.'

He also who had received the one talent came forward, saying, 'Master, I knew you to be a hard man, reaping where you did not sow, and gathering where you scattered no seed, so I was afraid, and I went and hid your talent in the ground. Here, you have what is yours.' But his master answered him, 'You wicked and slothful servant! You knew that I reap where I have not sown and gather where I scattered no seed? Then you ought to have invested my money with the bankers, and at my coming I should have received what was my own with interest. So take the talent from him and give it to him who has the ten talents. For to everyone who has more will be given, and he will have an abundance. But from the one who has not, even what he has will be taken away. And cast the worthless servant into the outer darkness. In that place there will be weeping and gnashing of teeth.

- Matthew 25:14-30 (ESV)

Do you wonder if God truly blesses hard work? Proverbs 28:19 (NLT) says, "A hard worker has plenty of food, but a person who chases fantasies ends up in poverty." This verse implies we must have wisdom when it comes to where we spend our time trying to make money. There is no easy path; hard work is part of the formula. Be careful of chasing schemes that promise abundance; fantasies bring poverty.

I've heard some people claim that it is more holy to be poor. That would imply that God programmed lack into us, and that He approves of us struggling. Taking a vow of poverty is a choice, but I don't believe that God wants His people to lack any good thing. In fact, quite the opposite is said in the Bible. John 10:10 (NKJV) says, "The thief does not come except to steal, and to kill, and to destroy. I have come that they may have life, and have it more abundantly."

Unfortunately, sometimes the Bible is used as a weapon against the wealthy. There is a story in Luke about the rich young ruler that is often pointed to as proof that God disapproves of wealthy people. People using that verse in that manner are taking it out of context and missing the bigger message.

You can read the story in Luke 18:18-25 (NIV). There is a rich young ruler who asks Jesus what he must do to inherit eternal life. He tells Jesus he has followed the commandments all his life. Jesus tells him to sell all he has and to follow Him. This makes the ruler sad, as he was very wealthy.

The well-used verse spoken by Jesus follows, and this is where people often stop. ""How hard it is for the rich to enter the kingdom of God! Indeed, it is easier for a camel to go through the eye of a needle than for someone who is rich to enter the kingdom of God." But if you read verses 26 and 27, and you understand the culture at the time, you would know that back then people thought you had to buy your way into heaven, and therefore rich people had an advantage.

But Jesus clarified that money means nothing for eternal life, that in fact what seemed impossible (making it to heaven as a poor person), was possible through His Father. Unfortunately for this rich young ruler, his wealth was his stumbling block. It didn't have to be that way. He had a toxic mindset about his money. But in no way does this story condemn all wealthy people.

I cannot begin to cover all of the verses in God's Word to demonstrate His mindset on money, but there is one more that I believe is worth pointing out. A verse in Proverbs highlights that leaving an inheritance is a good thing, in fact we are to do so for a couple of generations past us.

"A good person leaves an inheritance for their children's children, but a sinner's wealth is stored up for the righteous." Proverbs 13:22 (NIV) This tells me that God sees our wealth-building as a blessing for generations in our family, and that we are to manage what He has given us well in order for us to hand it down.

5. How much is enough money?

Including this question is less about providing you with my viewpoint and more about provoking the thought and getting you to consider it. Do you have a belief that people should only have a certain amount of money…that they don't need more than that? Do you have an idea of what "enough money" means in your life?

When you read about the Jewish Havdalah ceremony in the next few pages, the concept of "filling your cup" will be discussed, and the meaning of "overflow". This is a very personal quest; how much money is enough for you? Even if you don't yet have an answer to that question, I can say for certain that you cannot answer that for someone else.

6. How do you make more money?

How do you approach the quest for money? Why do you want more money? How do you make more money? If you look at this question philosophically, the answer is simply *serve more people*. We attract money in our purpose when we provide value to others; when we solve a problem for them or create something that they need. Therefore, to make more money, we must serve a great number of people with our purpose. I know this seems counterintuitive, but money follows a servant's heart.

Serving more people isn't just the idea of growing your client base as a business owner. In fact, as an employee you should consider your employer your customer. Employees who look at their work the same way as entrepreneurs look at their businesses, move out of the "wage slave" mindset and into greater opportunities.

In his book, *Business Secrets from the Bible: Spiritual Success Strategies for Financial Abundance,*[1] Rabbi Daniel Lapin says, "The company that writes your paycheck every two weeks is not your employer; they are your customer. Adopt this mindset and everything changes. You are free from the daily grind—free to grow your business and serve your customers, your fellow man."

Examine your motives behind your desire for more money. Wanting money just for money's sake will not work in the long run. As described in Chapter 5, there must be pure motives behind our purpose and therefore in our provision. There has been a lot of buzz in recent years about discovering your WHY. It is said if you know your WHY, God will give you the HOW. May I add, however, that you need to examine your WHY and make sure it contains a spirit of serving and a pure heart. James 4:2-3 (NIV) says, "You do not have because you do not ask God. When you ask, you do not receive, because you ask with wrong motives, that you may spend what you get on your pleasures."

Wanting more abundance in your life means you must play a bigger game with a stronger money mindset. It is often a matter of perspective. Think of money as a stream that is flowing, and you are standing in the middle of that stream. Money is always either flowing *to* you or *away* from you. How do you change your circumstances? How do you get money to flow to you instead of away from you? You turn around and face upstream…you change your perspective!

One way you do that is to understand how God brings us more abundance…is it a check in the mail? Not usually. Does it just show up in our bank account once we fix our toxic mindset? Not likely. Matthew 7:7-8 (NIV) says, "Ask and it will be given to you; seek and you will find; knock and the door will be opened to you. For everyone who asks receives; the one who seeks finds; and to the one who knocks, the door will be opened."

Ask and it will be given to you. What will be given to you? If you ask for more money, will that be given to you? I submit that God does not necessarily hand you more money, but rather gives you the opportunity to make more money in the form of something specific for you and your purpose. That is the HOW that God gives you, and you take advantage of that opportunity and turn it into money. But if we keep expecting God to show up for us only in the way we think He will or He should, we will miss it. I don't know who wrote this story, but it communicates my point well.

God Will Save Me

A terrible storm came into a town and local officials sent out an emergency warning that the riverbanks would soon overflow and flood the nearby homes. They ordered everyone in the town to evacuate immediately.

A faithful Christian man heard the warning and decided to stay, saying to himself, "I will trust God and if I am in danger, then God will send a divine miracle to save me."

The neighbors came by his house and said to him, "We're leaving and there is room for you in our car, please come with us!" But the man declined. "I have faith that God will save me."

As the man stood on his porch watching the water rise up the steps, a man in a canoe paddled by and called to him, "Hurry and come into my canoe, the waters are rising quickly!" But the man again said, "No thanks, God will save me."

The floodwaters rose higher pouring water into his living room and the man had to retreat to the second floor. A police motorboat came by and saw him at the window. "We will come up and rescue you!" they shouted. But the man refused, waving them off saying, "Use your time to save someone else! I have faith that God will save me!"

The floodwaters rose higher and higher and the man had to climb up to his rooftop.

A helicopter spotted him and dropped a rope ladder. A rescue officer came down the ladder and pleaded with the man, "Grab my hand and I will pull you up!" But the man STILL refused, folding his arms tightly to his body. "No thank you! God will save me!"

Shortly after, the house broke up and the floodwaters swept the man away and he drowned.

When in Heaven, the man stood before God and asked, "I put all of my faith in You. Why didn't You come and save me?"

And God said, "Son, I sent you a warning. I sent you a car. I sent you a canoe. I sent you a motorboat. I sent you a helicopter. What more were you looking for?"

This story illustrates a biblical concept from Malachi 3:10 of how God provides for his people, of which I believe many are unaware. Most churchgoers know the following verse, as it relates to tithing:

Bring all the tithes into the storehouse,
That there may be food in My house,
And try Me now in this,
Says the Lord of Hosts,
If I will not open for you the windows of heaven
*And pour out for you such a **blessing***
That there will not be room enough to receive it.

What is fascinating is that the word **blessing** in Strong's Concordance[2] is defined as "benediction" (Strong's 1293), which means "an utterance; a good word". Another way to say this is "If I will not open for you the windows of heaven and pour out for you such **a good word** that there will not be room enough to receive it."

What is a good word? It is personal insight, an idea, something specific given to you that fits your purpose and your situation. It is direction, guidance, and the best advice you'll ever receive! It is "legal" insider information and the idea that will change your life. It is all of that and some of that. Whatever it is, it is specifically for you, a good word which will bring with it increase.

What do we do with that good word? We act on it, and the increase comes. From that increase we sow more finances where God asks us to, and more blessings, or good words, come to us. The cycle goes on, continuously, as long as we play our role. This is what we call connecting our sowing to our reaping. Ever wonder why money you have sown hasn't brought you a harvest? Maybe it did but you missed it. It was probably a good word for you to act on!

Understand this biblical pattern so you can see the results in your financial life:

✓   God asks us to give

✓   The windows of heaven open

✓   An idea or concept that fits our life personally is spoken through that window

✓   We act on it

✓   More finances come in

✓   And the pattern continues…

What are you looking for to save you financially? God is sending you cars, boats, helicopters, and all kinds of "good words" to help you turn your money situation around, but are you missing it? Are you looking for the wrong thing?

There is only one way to make money: finding out what other people want or need and then providing those things to as many of our fellow humans as possible. This is the only way to earn money, no matter your occupation.

– Rabbi Daniel Lapin

I find the traditional Jewish faith fascinating as it relates to wealth creation. The tenants of their faith and the way they raise their children is typically with a very healthy, positive mindset about money, rooted in their scriptures and traditions. Studying what they believe about money is quite revealing.

In his book, *Thou Shall Prosper,*[3] Rabbi Daniel Lapin describes how the financial wisdom in the ancient Jewish faith is a recipe for success. The mindset about money and business in the Jewish tradition has helped that ethnic group win with money over the past few centuries even under the greatest odds and pressures.

Rabbi Lapin describes a special service, called the Havdalah, that is conducted after the end of the Sabbath and as the work week is to begin the next day. The service is recited over a cup of wine, as that wine is poured and runs over into the saucer beneath it. As Rabbi Lapin says, "This observance divides the Sabbath from the upcoming work week and asks God to increase both the families' offspring and their wealth. It also highlights their hands, as if to beseech blessing on the work of those very hands."

There are three things about this sacred service that I find intriguing and illuminating in regard to money mindset:

1. God is asked to bless their hands for the upcoming work week in order that they may be financially productive. This further emphasizes that God approves of money and desires for us to prosper, and that it is OK to ask God for finances! It also underscores that hard work and business are positive endeavors to be admired.

2. As the wine is being poured into the cup, the principle that each person needs to provide for their family first before helping others is highlighted. If you cannot or will not provide for the needs of your family, you have no ability (and certainly no business) helping others. It isn't selfishness, it is a matter of healthy priorities as it relates to wealth creation and money management. It is not shameful to attend to your needs first, but it is seen as a moral obligation.

This directive is also in the Christian faith. 1 Timothy 5:8 (NIV) says, "Anyone who does not provide for their relatives, and especially for their own household, has denied the faith and is worse than an unbeliever." We must get our financial priorities in order so we may position ourselves for increase.

3. Being able to provide for your family first has to do with the size of your "cup". As the wine is being poured into the cup, what is within it represents meeting the needs of your family (and this is where I believe your tithe is), and the overflow is used to bless others. The question that is so important to answer is "what is the right size of your cup?".

No matter where you are financially, you must decide the size of your cup. What does that mean? What is my lifestyle like? How much do I spend on personal needs? What kind of car do I drive? Where do I live? What do I spend on vacations? And the list goes on. The size of your cup is influenced by your choices as well as the needs and number of people in your immediate family. Also, it may be impacted by other extended family members who, for whatever reason, genuinely require your financial help.

Who decides on the size of the cup? You do, with God's help. If you are married, it is you, your spouse, and God. No one else can make that determination. No one else has the right to tell you that your cup is too big or is too small. It is between you and God. He helps you determine the size, and then He helps you fill it to overflowing.

Everyone has a different cup size, and your size changes along with life's circumstances. If you are just starting in your career, you need to decide the size of your cup so you can fill it, and still have overflow. It probably isn't very big at this point. If you are a multi-millionaire, though, you still need to decide the size of your cup! What should your lifestyle look like? How much do you spend on your family and meeting their needs? Decide that with God, and then have fun distributing the overflow to bless others. This really is a visual for the exercise of budgeting, but it is rooted in spirituality.

By realizing that everyone has a different size cup, it releases us from comparison and envy. We are not free to comment on how someone else spends their money, as we are not part of that decision. Our eyes should be on our situation and our requests to God should be to show us how to meet our family's needs, what the size of our "cup" should be, and that He would fill it to overflowing. It is that increase and outpouring which will come back to you ten-fold and allow you to continue to sow financially in ways that changes lives. That is our over-arching purpose, remember - to change someone's life for the better. Money can do that.

Money is only a tool. It will take you wherever you wish, but it will not replace you as the driver.

– Ayn Rand

The road to wealth and abundance is laden with mindset traps, or excuses we use to keep us from walking in the prosperity we were designed to experience. No matter what stage you find yourself in life - just starting, starting over, or experiencing growth and maintaining in your finances, you must have a healthy relationship with your money and an understanding of the role it should play in your life.

There is a misconception that people who have "more than enough money" (however that is defined) do not struggle with a toxic money mindset. That's just not true. Working on getting rid of limiting money beliefs is not solely for the purpose of attracting more money; it is also so you can be a good steward of what you've been given.

Instead of just working on a financial plan for your life, consider adding a spiritual element - work on improving your money mindset and eliminating any toxic beliefs that are holding you back. Change your family tree by breaking those negative cycles and instead handing down healthy money mindsets to your children. Allow your money to work for good in your life and those around you.

✛

BELIEFS ABOUT MONEY

One has to work hard for money
I think about money a lot
Money is not easy to come by
I don't need money to be happy
I am careful what I spend money on
A successful person makes a lot of money
Never lend money
Money is there to be spent
Never borrow money
Money solves all problems
Buying things makes me feel good
It's not what you make but what you keep
Money makes you happy
God wants me to have money
Money is a scorecard
Money is for me to enjoy
The one with the most toys wins
God will provide, I don't need to think about money
My spouse will provide, I don't need to think about money
There is never enough money
I don't deserve a lot of money when others have less
The more money someone has, the smarter they are
Things would get better if I had more money
You have to earn everything you have
It's extravagant to spend money on myself
Giving people money ruins them
Money is good
I spend a lot of time looking for deals/coupons
Money is evil
It is better to save than spend
Money is behind all the good things in the world

Money funds all the bad things in the world
Profit is evil
Money never comes easy, except the lottery
There is virtue in living with less money
I don't need to leave an inheritance
It is better to give than receive
Either rich or happy
Money tends to corrupt people
I'm not good with money
I could never have too much money
My family has never been rich
I'll never have enough money
It's not fair that other people have more money
The more money someone else has, the less there is for me
Everyone should have the same amount of money
People should work for their money
Money powers the world
If I had a lot of money, it would be hard for me to trust what people
want from me
Money changes people
Wealthy people tend to take their money for granted
It is rude to talk about money
Rich people are not honest
I'm uncomfortable talking about money or how much I make
I'm jealous of people with money
Businesses exploit workers
The rich get richer and the poor get poorer
My boss makes too much money

MINDSET SHIFTS

1. Work through the list of limiting beliefs in this chapter. Without hesitating, circle those thoughts that you have regarding money. Add any that are missing.

2. Take your top three limiting beliefs about money and work through them using the fourteen-step process in Chapter 4.

3. Determine the size of your financial cup. This is not just a budget, but a determination of how you want to live. Do this with prayer, and with your spouse if you are married.

4. Plan for the overflow in your life. How will you put that money into action to change other's lives?

5. Use the mantras at the end of this chapter to begin to change your thought patterns regarding money. Add additional statements that are relevant to you.

MONEY AFFIRMATIONS

1. I am grateful for the blessings God has given me.
2. It is not the amount of money I have but my attitude towards it that blesses my life.
3. I am a magnet for ideas that generate money.
4. Prosperity and favor are drawn to me.
5. I have an abundance mindset, not a poverty mindset.
6. I am worthy of making more money.
7. I am an effective manager of the money God entrusts to me and I ensure my family's needs are met.
8. I choose more, I choose better, I choose greater in my life.
9. I understand that God brings me more money by way of ideas, opportunities, and relationships and I can recognize His prompting.
10. I will leave an inheritance that will bless my children and generations beyond them.
11. I am diligent to bless others from the overflow in my life.
12. Just because someone else has more money does not mean I will have less. There is no limit of money in God's economy.

_____

_____

_____

CHAPTER EIGHT
The Blessing of Failure

The greatest teacher, failure is.

— Master Yoda, The Last Jedi

Each time he said, "My grace is all you need. My power works best in weakness." So now I am glad to boast about my weaknesses, so that the power of Christ can work through me. That's why I take pleasure in my weaknesses, and in the insults, hardships, persecutions, and troubles that I suffer for Christ. For when I am weak, then I am strong.

— 2 Corinthians 12:9-10 (NLT)

The Blessing of Failure

*T*his, the last chapter, is actually the *first* chapter of this book that I completed; I started by focusing on failure. That could seem a less than uplifting way to start writing a mindset book until you realize that looking back on our failures and understanding how God can create beauty from ashes, generates an excitement that propels you into all the other mindset categories with more intentional force and focus. My failure is part of the fabric of my success, and one needs the other.

Also, I leave you with the topic of failure as the ending to this book because I know that as you push to master your mindset, focus on your purpose, and run after your destiny, you will experience failure. It is your response to that failure that determines what happens next. If you are shaking your head right now in disagreement or if you believe that speaking about failure will bring it into your life, perhaps you need to dig further. Perhaps you are afraid of failure. But should you be?

Failure is not an option; it is a necessity.

During your journey, you will be tested. You've heard the saying that nothing worth having comes easy.

Most people recoil at the idea that they need to fail at some point, that they must fail to truly succeed. Fear of failure is such a strong emotion that it keeps many from walking in their true purpose and experiencing the life God intended them to have.

How many ground-breaking, ultra-creative, life-changing ideas have gone unrealized because of the fear of failure? How many dreams have been sidelined and talents hidden due to a desire to avoid feeling the sting of defeat?

Fear is our enemy, but failure is not. But it's such a "dirty" word, even the Webster definition makes you want to run and hide. That definition includes phrases like "lack of success; falling short". How about the synonyms to "failure" - those will really make you wince...here are some of those:

Attack	Bankruptcy	Breakdown	Collapse
Decline	Defeat	Deficiency	Deterioration
Loss	Bomb	Downfall	Fiasco
Flop	Implosion	Inadequacy	Lemon
Loser	Washout	Wreck	Sinking Ship

Tough words. The one that stood out to me was ATTACK. Failure does feel like an attack. Does God allow it in our life? Yes, I believe He does at times. I've told you before, be prepared to experience attacks in your area of gifting and purpose. Don't be surprised when it comes, in fact often I believe it can be a confirmation that you are where God wants you to be and you must fight through the resistance.

Let's be honest, none of us want to hear that, after all, walking in our destiny is like floating on a cloud and tiptoeing through a field of tulips, right? Not even close. Although there are moments it feels almost magical, and inspiring moments that give us glimpses into the future that keep us going through the hard times.

God uses failures and challenges to grow us, to prune us, to mold us into who He intends us to be so our destiny can be fulfilled. This is why James tells us, "My brethren, count it all joy when you fall into various trials, knowing that the testing of your faith produces patience. But let patience have its perfect work, that you may be perfect and complete, lacking nothing." James 1:2-4 (NKJV)

Failure is a necessary element of the human experience. Yet most of us learn from a young age to shun failure and to fear its presence in our lives. Our society has drawn such a strong connection of shame to failure that countless lives have been ruined over the inability to get past a failure - public or private - and the sense of judgment, labeling, self-condemnation, and embarrassment that follows. But are we actually shunning something that can eventually lead us to success?

Failure is not the opposite of success, it's part of success.

– Arianna Huffington

When my husband and I lost our first business during the recession of 2008, it was painful in a way that is hard to describe. Not only did our hard work, hopes, dreams, investments, and more appear to go down the drain, but with it our very name and it seemed our reputation. That was the mindset I had to fight. Those were the thoughts I needed to oppose.

It wasn't easy – suddenly I looked around and all I saw was failure, and I had never failed that big before. It took a lot of prayer, self-reflection, and frankly just holding on to God each day in order to make it to the other side. The failure threatened to sideline me, stop me from trying again, make me feel defeated, and even challenged the future of my marriage.

The fear generated by that failure wanted to move in with me, to be my constant companion, and to suffocate my desire to dream in anything again. I had to be careful to what voices I listened and with whom I sought counsel. I will admit, short of my dad's untimely death, it was one of the hardest times of my life. It wasn't just a failure that happened in a moment and was over – we had to pick up the pieces and deal with the side effects and the fall-out for years to come.

It was out of this failure that a very successful business was formed as well as my personal purpose and mission, but had I chosen to give in and give up, that business would not be here today, and I would not be writing this book.

Often, I had to struggle with the lie in my head that told me I could never be an entrepreneur and mindset coach if I had a failed business! What did I have to offer? How could anyone take me seriously? Wouldn't they just be looking for my successes to validate my worthiness?

To fight that, I actually started my coaching business soon after going through this experience. My husband and I built a company from nothing, took it to the prestigious Inc. 5000 List of America's Fastest Growing Companies, and then it died. Hard. That experience, that story, has more advice, cautionary tales, recommendations, and guidance in it than anything I could conjure up on my own. So now I embrace it.

Understand there are still days that the enemy tries to get me to feel condemned, to wonder why, to question what we did…I fight those thoughts. The more I do, the less I have them. I'm not suggesting that I always handled the failure perfectly, but I certainly learned more from it than from my successes.

My dad encouraged us to fail. Growing up, he would ask us what we failed at that week. If we didn't have something, he would be disappointed. It changed my mindset at an early age that failure is not the outcome, failure is not trying. Don't be afraid to fail.

— Sara Blakely, billionaire founder of Spanx

Failure doesn't always show up in dramatic ways like losing a business or a career, sometimes it's just daily demoralizing adversity and resistance that keeps hitting at us again and again in small batches.

Ironically, as I write this chapter my husband and I experienced a day full of adversity in one of our most thriving businesses. It was a test for sure: our expensive, main work truck broke down two hours from the office on a busy New York expressway, we received an unfair bad review online, and our two top guys quit to pursue other opportunities.

Let me also mention while my husband and I were meeting at a coffee shop to discuss growth and strategy for that business, we both received parking tickets for staying too long in an unmetered area (all of this happening over the period of 6 hours).

OK, so big deal – parking tickets. The other items are a bit more serious, yes, but of course we can work through them. But it is all a form of resistance meant to sideline us, stymy us, and make us question ourselves even for a short period of time. I'm sure you have similar stories.

The size of the adversity or challenge isn't what is most daunting; rather, it seems to be that layering effect when you keep taking punches in succession and feel like you can't breathe, and your feet are unsteady. It's that pit-in-your-stomach feeling that things are suddenly not going your way, that fear that rises up that this may be the start of bigger problems. Then you begin to think back to more difficult times in your life and you wonder if you are headed again in that direction of a season of challenge and pain.

Doubt and uncertainty are always waiting around the corner to entice you to listen to their voices, to engage with them, to believe their lies and to buy into their negativity. Sometimes it doesn't take much for us to entertain these enemies of our mindset much longer than we should. It's that resistance we talked about in an earlier chapter.

Giving into the resistance we experience means we can lose our way and become stuck in the adversity rather than learning from it, rising above it, and moving forward in spite of it.

The main difference between the wise man and a fool

is that a fool's mistakes never teach him anything.

- Unknown

I often say that I enjoy so much more speaking with an entrepreneur who has failed at one time (which frankly are most if being honest), as we have so much in common. I believe that is part of my testimony, part of my mission, and the very reason I am a great entrepreneur and mindset coach. I've been there, done that…it's not just theory to me. Some of the most powerful words spoken to a heart in pain are "I understand. It also happened to me, I survived, and you can too."

It's really how you handle your failure that makes all the difference. How you respond to it, and how you use it to move you forward and to help others. Then failure becomes an asset.

Train yourself to look at failure differently, to consider it as part of the success formula.

In the book *Psycho-Cybernetics*,[1] Dr. Maxwell Maltz, in illustrating how the brain learns, urges "Do not be afraid of making mistakes, or of temporary failures. All servo-mechanisms achieve a goal by negative feedback, or by going forward, making mistakes, and immediately correcting course. Skill learning of any kind is accomplished by trial and error, mentally correcting aim after an error, until a 'successful' motion, movement, or performance has been achieved. After that, further learning, and continued success, is accomplished by *forgetting the past errors, and remembering the successful response,* so that it can be imitated."

Lest you think I am writing something to make you feel warm and cozy about your mistakes, understand that I don't believe we should embrace making the SAME mistakes time and again. This is where our learning mechanism must kick in, along with discipline and growth, in order to benefit from our mistakes and turn them into successes. As you have likely heard often, doing the same thing over and over and expecting different results is the definition of insanity.

As Dr. Maltz says, "Continued success is accomplished by forgetting the past errors, and remembering the successful response, so that it can be imitated."

You may have failed, but you are not a failure.

That's what you did. That's not who you are.

— Joel Olsteen

If every professional athlete turned his or her inevitable losses into judgments about their worthiness or ability, they would never progress nor have the opportunity to rise to the top of their sport. If every inventor gave up out of frustration and self-condemnation when their first attempt at innovation failed, we'd have almost none of the discoveries that make our quality of life what it is. If every salesperson took their first "no" as a reflection of their lack of business ability...you get the picture.

I believe you need to learn how to lose well before you develop the honorable and healthy attitude reflected in winning well. In losses or failures, harshly blaming yourself actually reflects the same kind of pride as a puffed-up and cocky response to winning.

In both cases, you are saying, "It's all about me. The outcome depends entirely on me."

Of course, personal responsibility is important, but the attitude that the results are 100% dependent on you cuts God out of the equation and can blind you from the necessary lessons both failure and success provide.

Don't get stuck at the place of your last broken dream.

– Pastor Donnie Rosa

When you face pressure from a failure or resistance, a vacuum is created in your life. You have to decide what to do next. You have the choice to fill that vacuum with "what if", "now what", and "what am I going to do", and stand paralyzed in the face of the fear.

Or, instead of staring frightened into the unknown, you can fill that space with faith, a healthy mindset, positive affirmations, and with action. You make a purposeful decision to see it as an opportunity to learn and take steps to move forward. Choose to see failure as your fuel to move you closer to your breakthrough.

So how will you respond?

I often tell my kids, "There actually is no failing. You either succeed or you learn."

Failure gives us a great opportunity to learn, unless our pride gets in the way. There are times that we bring failure into our lives. Admit it, sometimes we make bad decisions from a lack of experience, immaturity, or just plain stubbornness. Our failures and adversity are not always the result of some powerful force against us, sometimes we just mess up! Other times God needs to wake us up or supernaturally push us off the wrong path.

Determine to learn from your mistakes and your failures. Embrace them and don't be ashamed. I learned more from my entrepreneurial trip-ups than I could ever learn from one of my college business classes.

Life is the best teacher, and failure can be the best motivator if you allow it to be. It's your choice. Respond the right way and don't give up. Failure actually provides us with much needed revelation about ourselves that can help us get back on track.

Teach children to not shrink from failure. I'm concerned society is raising a generation of failure-adverse kids who think they are entitled to have a life that makes them feel good and safe just because they deserve it. Why would they step out of their comfort zone and reach for something bigger? Why risk the pain of failure if life owes you anyway?

Truly that's another book on not raising entitled children. But it is applicable to our discussion of failure. Our kids need not shy away from the possibility of failure in order to reach for their dreams and find their true purpose.

Please, if you have influence over any child in your life, teach them this. Be the one who encouraged them to try, never quit, and not fear failure. Our world will be better for it, and someday they may attribute their very success to your wisdom and guidance.

There is no elevator to success.

You have to take the stairs.

- Unknown

On a recent trip to see their Nana and Grandpa, my four kids watched the Rocky movie series every night after a long day playing in the water and sun. Now that I see these movies as an adult, it is easy to laugh at the cheesiness and roll your eyes at the inevitable ending. But every time Rocky got up and turned his failures into successes, I would get teary-eyed and my heart would jump a little.

I'm not sure my young kids could appreciate the symbolism in those stories to the degree that I did, but Rocky would get pummeled again and again…his dreams would seem to be lost, his future in question. But there was something in him, an unlikely hero from the streets of Philadelphia, that made him get BACK UP. He would take a beating and get back up.

In one movie, both boxers were on the ground, and the winner was determined simply by the one WHO GOT BACK UP. Rocky was exhausted, bloodied, hurting, and demoralized…he had every reason to give up. His wife and his coach were cheering him on outside the ring "get up, get up!". As he rose slowly and wobbled on his feet, you felt your heart soar and the crowd went wild. Simply getting up from his impending defeat changed his destiny and turned what looked like the end of the story into a new chapter. But it wasn't simple…it was painfully difficult!

I honestly think it is better to be a failure at something you love

than to be a success at something you hate.

– George Burns

We tend to hero worship those whom we see as great successes in business, sports, politics, entertainment, and other public stages without fully understanding their story and the failures they endured on their way to success (and likely the smaller failures they face ongoing in life).

I have to believe that most of you reading this have heard the stories summarized below, but they bear repeating, especially if you are facing a recent failure or are stymied because of your fear of failure. These are simply a sampling of stories of failure preceding success. While these are recognizable names, if you look around your community there are certainly neighbors, friends, relatives and other everyday people who have their own inspiring stories of success and failure. We should be just as motivated by the "every man" stories as well.

The Bible says that God is not a respecter of persons (Acts 10:34), so what He has done for others, whether that is Abraham Lincoln or your neighbor John Smith, He can do for you! That's why stories of overcoming the odds should always give us hope and inspiration.

President Abraham Lincoln

A seeming failure at 51 – Abraham Lincoln had suffered depression, several election defeats, two bankruptcies, a nervous breakdown, and the death of his fiancée. While all of the circumstances in his life seemed to prove otherwise, he had a sense of destiny that pushed him to continue in the face of repeated failures and he summoned the courage to run for President. Lincoln changed history and blessed this nation greatly.

"I am not bound to win; I am bound to be true. I am not bound to succeed, but I am bound to live up to the light that I have."

– Abraham Lincoln

Michael Jordan, Athlete

Even though he is now recognized as one of the best athletes professional sports has ever seen, Jordan was cut from his high school basketball team as a sophomore. While others may have viewed that as a reason to quit and give up their dream, Jordan pushed forward, worked harder, and made the team the next year. He was unwilling to let go of the pursuit of the giftings he knew had been put inside of him, and his diligence paid off tremendously.

"I've missed more than 9,000 shots in my career. I've lost almost 300 games. 26 times, I've been trusted to take the game winning shot and missed. I've failed over and over and over again in my life. And that is why I succeed." - Michael Jordan

Thomas Edison, Inventor

Holding over 1,000 U.S. patents, Thomas Edison invented well-known items such as the photograph, light bulb, and motion picture camera. Edison was told by his teachers in school that he was too stupid to learn anything and was fired from his first two jobs. Undaunted, he went on to create a company where failures were celebrated and there were no limits put on creativity and innovation. Edison saw failure as an essential part of invention.

"I have not failed. I've just found 10,000 ways that won't work. Many of life's failures are people who did not realize how close they were to success when they gave up." - Thomas A. Edison

Sylvester Stallone, Actor/Writer/Director

After complications during his birth, Stallone sustained injuries that made the lower left part of his face slightly paralyzed, accounting for his famous snarl and slurred speech. His parents had a troubled marriage and he found himself bouncing between foster homes. At one point, he was homeless. The success of the Rocky film series did not come about easily. Stallone wrote the script himself in 20 hours and was rejected again and again by potential buyers. Once he began to get some offers, he held out until he had one that included him playing the lead role. He refused to settle.

"I am not the richest, smartest or most talented person in the world, but I succeed because I keep going and going and going."- Sylvester Stallone

Henry Ford, Inventor and Entrepreneur

Ford failed and went broke five times before he succeeded. He trusted in his ideas when no one else did, and his persistence allowed him to become the father of modern transportation. Ford also invented the modern assembly line which transformed the manufacturing industry as we know it.

"Failure is the opportunity to begin again more intentionally."

- Henry Ford

Vera Wang, Fashion Designer

As a young girl Wang dreamed of becoming an Olympic ice skater and spent her childhood and adolescence training for the sport. Eventually she had to face the fact that she wasn't going to rise to the top of the sport and made the difficult decision to quit. She then pursued a writing career in fashion which stalled when she was passed up for an important promotion at Vogue. This all pushed her to eventually start a fashion line, becoming the biggest name in couture wedding dress design.

"No matter how bad things get, no matter how discouraged I feel, no matter how much of a failure I feel like ... I try to believe there's a reason, there's a process, and there's a learning experience."- Vera Wang

Walt Disney, Entrepreneur

While he is now synonymous with unlimited creativity and entrepreneurial success, it is worth noting that Disney was once fired from a newspaper because he was told he "lacked creativity". Pushing ahead, he formed his first animation company, which he was forced to close in failure. He reached bottom, was out of money, and found his way to Hollywood. Still, he faced more criticism and failure until his first film, *Snow White and the Seven Dwarfs*, became popular in 1937. The rest is history and frankly his success mind-boggling. Imagine if Disney had stopped after those early failures. We can learn from him not to quit in the face of repeated failures. Fight for the dream God has put into your heart.

"All the adversity I've had in my life, all my troubles and

obstacles, have strengthened me... You may not realize it when it happens, but a kick in the teeth may be the best thing in the world for you." - Walt Disney

King David, King of Israel

The story of King David shows us that failure and bad choices don't disqualify you, even though you may feel unqualified. God says that King David was a man after His own heart, and God chose him as a shepherd boy to be the great king of Israel. David's successes are many, beginning with the slaying of Goliath. But his failures were just as dramatic as David allowed sin to creep into his life and he became a murderer and adulterer. So much of David's story reflects the complex nature of man's life and proves to us that even in our failings God can use us in a mighty way.

Joseph, son of Jacob

When favored son Joseph shared his dream with his brothers (Genesis 37), he clearly didn't think through the fact that they would not be so thrilled to hear that he saw them bowing down to him. They hated him all the more, and soon Joseph found himself sold into slavery and taken to Egypt. A faithful slave, Joseph was unfairly thrown in prison for standing up for his morals and resisting his master's wife. All of this failure and adversity was actually setting him up to eventually run the country of Egypt and save it and his family from famine. The failure was necessary and had Joseph given up, his brilliant destiny would have never been realized. If you aren't familiar with this story, it's a great read.

Failure is not final unless you give up and give in.

Fail your way forward.

Winston Churchill is famously known for saying, "Never give in. Never give in. Never, never, never, never - in nothing, great or small, large or petty - never give in, except to convictions of honour and good sense. Never yield to force. Never yield to the apparently overwhelming might of the enemy."

This never-quit attitude certainly inspired a country at war and since has been often misquoted as simply "Never, never, never give up." It's certainly a message we all need to hear.

However, while I do agree with Churchill and the inspirational sentiment behind the words, I think we also have to guard against confusing "not quitting" with holding on too tightly to something God wants to move out of your life in order for something better to materialize.

Don't become comfortable with quitting,

instead learn how to be good at ending well.

A dear friend of mine once suggested a great book, *Necessary Endings*[2] by Dr. Henry Cloud, when discussing an organization that was perpetually experiencing hard times and lack of progression. While the book focuses largely on issues in business, it also has applications in our personal lives. The premise is that many of us have not been taught to end things well, or even know when they need to end.

First, let's agree that everything, good and bad, has an end. Just read Ecclesiastes 3:1-8 if you need to meditate on seasons and the inevitability of change. If it is the appointed time for something to end or a season to change, I for one would like to be a part of that process rather than futilely fighting it.

Is deciding to proactively end or just allowing something to end the same as quitting? If I advocate never giving up, then how can I also advocate the concept of embracing healthy endings?

It's not the same. Consider the definitions in Webster's Dictionary:

> **Quit:**[3] *to cease normal, expected, or necessary action;* **to admit defeat**
>
> **End:**[4] *cessation of a course of action, pursuit, or activity*

In many ways the definitions are similar, with at least one very stark contrast: "to quit" also means "to admit defeat". The spirit behind each word and the connected intention is very different.

Quitting is a defeatist, sometimes dramatic reaction in which the initiator throws his or her hands up in the air and gives up. Ending something, however, is an intentional, well-thought out decision that allows necessary change and bigger and better things to materialize.

Ending something well is not quitting. Don't quit but develop the skill to know when something needs to end and muster the courage to do so and positively be part of that process.

Dr. Cloud tells us, "When we fail to end things well, we are destined to repeat the mistakes that keep us from moving on. We choose the same kind of dysfunctional person or demoralizing job again. Not learning our lessons and proactively dealing with them, we make the same business or personal mistakes over and over."

The clenched fist is incapable of accepting new things.

Let go, open your hand.

Do you see endings as a problem? Are you holding on too tightly to something that needs to pass out of your life or your business? It's hard, I admit, to end something you have invested in heavily in one way or another.

Yes, we can use the word failure to apply to an ending - I hope by now you don't see it as a dirty word. Rather, one of the best skills you can develop is the ability to fail well. Bringing or allowing an ending to something, seeing it, accepting it, and moving on to better seasons.

Good business leaders must make these decisions often. Sometimes it's not bringing a complete end to a project, idea, or even a company, but it is a change in direction that is needed. No matter the size of the "end", not ending something at the right time will hamper your growth in that area.

I believe God often gives us the time and space to come to the realization of a necessary end ourselves, and then eventually when we refuse to acknowledge the need for it and champion that ending ourselves, He will bring it to fruition Himself. Ouch. But it is always for our greater good. Always.

If you can see endings as a natural course of life, you will open yourself up to greater opportunities and success. It's OK to see an ending as a failure, for now we know that failure is necessary, and that closed doors push us to find the open window.

Dr. Cloud says, "Endings are a part of every aspect of life. When done well, the seasons of life are negotiated, and the proper endings lead to the end of pain, greater growth, personal and business goals reached and better lives. Endings bring hope. When done poorly, bad outcomes happen, good opportunities are lost, and misery either remains or is repeated. Let's get empowered to choose the necessary endings, execute them well, and get to the better results we all desire."

Don't quit; rather, know when to end things well. Respond correctly to failure, adversity and pressure, and you will always benefit from the experience. Your endings and your failures are your badges of honor, not your successes, as long as you end well.

When you experience failure, don't let fear take hold. Stop. Breathe. Watch your words. Renew your thoughts. Pray. Stay in peace. Look for the opportunity. Problem-solve. Ask for help. TRUST. Don't give up. End what needs to end. Pray more. Allow God to be in control. TRUST more. Let go. Heal. Grow. Repeat.

✝

MINDSET SHIFTS

1. How does the fear of failure show up in your life? Think about specific examples where it held you back and consider what you may have done differently.

2. Write down your three "biggest" failures. What did you learn from them? How did they point you to a better path? If you don't see the positive side of the failure now, challenge yourself to re-write the story and embrace the failure.

3. Is there something in your life right now that you want to achieve but the fear of failure is holding you back? How could life change for you if you face that fear head-on? You've likely already mapped out the possibilities for failure in your head, but what if you succeed? What does that look like?

4. Over the next 30 days, take one step each day towards a goal that is important to you, but you have avoided because of the fear of failure. Commit yourself to accomplishing the daily task and push back against the fear as it tries to stop you. Continue this process until the fear fades and your confidence grows.

5. Is there anything in your life that needs to "end well"? Are there things that you are holding onto for fear of letting them go? How might your life change if you allow this sometimes necessary process to happen?

THE MAN IN THE ARENA

Excerpt from the speech "Citizenship in a Republic"
by Theodore Roosevelt
Delivered at the Sorbonne, Paris, France on April 23, 1910

"It is not the critic who counts;
not the man who points out how the strong man stumbles,
or where the doer of deeds could have done them better.

The credit belongs to the man who is actually in the arena,
whose face is marred by dust and sweat and blood;
who strives valiantly; who errs, who comes short again and again,
because there is no effort without error and shortcoming;
but who does actually strive to do the deeds;
who knows great enthusiasms, the great devotions;
who spends himself in a worthy cause; who at the best knows
in the end the triumph of high achievement,
and who at the worst, if he fails, at least fails
while daring greatly, so that his place shall never be
with those cold and timid souls who neither
know victory nor defeat."

The Blessing of Failure

Just say where you want to go and believe that it will be so. Because every journey begins with a desire to go somewhere and do something and if you have a desire then you also have the power to make it happen.

— Jon Gordon, The Energy Bus

- fini -

Endnotes

Chapter 1

1 Dr. Jason Lisle. "God and Natural Law." *Answers Magazine* (August 28, 2006), https://answersingenesis.org/is-god-real/god-natural-law/

2 Natural. 2019. In Merriam-Webster.com. Retrieved March 1, 2019, from https://www.merriam-webster.com/dictionary/natural

3 Law. 2019. In Merriam-Webster.com. Retrieved March 1, 2019, from https://www.merriam-webster.com/dictionary/law

4 Napoleon Hill. https://www.youtube.com/watch?time_continue=1&v=2hA-7aq6OXI

5 Humility. 2019. In Merriam-Webster.com. Retrieved March 1, 2019, from https://www.merriam-webster.com/dictionary/humility

6 Hubris. 2019. In Merriam-Webster.com. Retrieved March 1, 2019, from https://www.merriam-webster.com/dictionary/hubris

Chapter 2

1 *Learning Mind.* https://www.learning-mind.com/the-human-heart-mind/

[2] Joseph Murphy, *The Power of Your Subconscious Mind* (New York: Prentice Hall Press, 2008).

[3] Ibid.

Chapter 3

[1] Steven Furtick, *Crash the Chatterbox* (Colorado Springs: Multnomah Books, 2014).

[2] Dr. Caroline Leaf, *Who Switched Off My Brain?* (Southlake: Switch On Your Brain International LLC, 2007).

Chapter 4

[1] Neuroplasticity. 2019. In Merriam-Webster.com. Retrieved March 1, 2019, from https://www.merriam-webster.com/dictionary/neuroplasticity

[2] Epigenetics. 2019. In Merriam-Webster.com. Retrieved March 1, 2019, from https://www.merriam-webster.com/dictionary/epigenetics

[3] Steven Pressfield, *The War of Art* (New York: Black Irish Entertainment LLC, 2002).

Chapter 5

[1] Dr. Myles Munroe, *In Pursuit of Purpose* (Shippensburg: Destiny Image Publishers, Inc., 2015).

[2] Marianne Williamson, *Return to Love* (New York: Harper One, 1996).

[3] Rick Warren, *The Purpose Driven Life* (New York: Zondervan, 2013).

Chapter 6

[1] James Strong, *The New Strong's Expanded Exhaustive Concordance of the Bible* (Nashville: Thomas Nelson, Inc., 2010).

[2] Krakowski, S. (2014, February). Finding Our Metron, *Entreprenuer*. Retrieved from https://www.entrepreneur.com/article/231582

Chapter 7

[1] Rabbi Daniel Lapin, *Business Secrets from the Bible* (Hoboken: John Wiley & Sons, Inc., 2014).

[2] James Strong, *The New Strong's Expanded Exhaustive Concordance of the Bible* (Nashville: Thomas Nelson, Inc., 2010).

[3] Rabbi Daniel Lapin, *Thou Shall Prosper* (Hoboken: John Wiley & Sons, Inc., 2010).

Chapter 8

[1] Dr. Maxwell Maltz, *Psycho-Cybernetics* (New York: Penguin Random House LLC, 2015).

[2] Dr. Henry Cloud, *Necessary Endings* (New York: Harper Collins, 2010).

[3] Quit. 2019. In Merriam-Webster.com. Retrieved March 1, 2019, from https://www.merriam-webster.com/dictionary/quit

[4] End. 2019. In Merriam-Webster.com. Retrieved March 1, 2019, from https://www.merriam-webster.com/dictionary/end